TEA PARTY REVIVAL

THE CONSCIENCE OF A CONSERVATIVE REBORN

D0838682

TEA PARTY REVIVAL

THE CONSCIENCE OF A CONSERVATIVE REBORN

The Tea Party Revolt Against
Unconstrained Spending and Growth
of the Federal Government

Dr. B. Leland Baker

Outskirts Press, Inc.
Denver, Colorado

Tea Party Revival: The Conscience of a Conservative Reborn
The Tea Party Revolt Against Unconstrained Spending and Growth of the Federal Government
All Rights Reserved.

Outskirts Press, Inc.
http://www.outskirtspress.com

ISBN: 978-1-4327-4917-0

Library of Congress Control Number: 2009938552

Outskirts Press and the "OP" logo are trademarks belonging to Outskirts Press, Inc.

PRINTED IN THE UNITED STATES OF AMERICA

Contents

On December 16, 1773, the Sons of Liberty threw
the "Boston Tea Party" to protest Britain's taxation
tyranny—*It is time for another Tea Party!*

TEA PARTY REVIVAL
OUR DEMANDS

- **We want** our unabridged freedoms as promised in the U.S. Constitution
- **We want** the president, the Congress, and courts to comply with the limits in the U.S. Constitution as the highest law of the land
- **We want** the courts to interpret, not make, laws
- **We want** an end to the robbery and redistribution of **our** personal property and wealth by Socialistic-Progressives
- **We want** the government to stop confiscating our wages for unconstitutional corporate welfare and foreign aid
- **We want** the large, wasteful federal government reduced to a level compliant with the U.S. Constitution and state rights
- **We want** the military to protect our borders, rather than foreign borders, in undeclared wars
- **We want** all elected officials to be subject to the same laws and penalties as our citizens
- **We want** a balanced budget and an end to deficit spending
- **We want** an audit, and then elimination, of the Federal Reserve
- **We want** each bill to be read thoroughly before it is voted upon
- **We want** all bills to quote the section and clause of the U.S. Constitution that provides legitimacy

PREFACE

In 1964, Barry M. Goldwater wrote *The Conscience of a Conservative,* identifying that the Republican Party was off course. Mr. Goldwater was a modern-day Thomas Jefferson with truly libertarian beliefs. The Jefferson and Goldwater political vision focused upon compliance with the United States Constitution. Constitutional compliance leads to smaller, limited government, which results in lower spending and consequently lower taxes.

These planks have been embedded in many election speeches, but not adhered to for the past 45 years. Deviation from Goldwater's vision of constitutional compliance has led to setbacks in the conservative movement and the irrelevance of the party elites.

Citizens who love liberty advocate for compliance with the U.S. Constitution. Tea Partiers are fiscal conservatives who want a limited federal government because we understand that deficit spending and ever-increasing debt is destroying our nation.

Tea Party Revival prescribes a way forward for citizens who prefer Tea Parties over the Republican or Democrat party. It is written in plain English instead of the double-speak of our Washington insiders and political elites. *Tea Party Revival* is also written for the politicians serving in Washington, D.C., who act as if they do not understand why American citizens are protesting; and it is dedicated to the one million Patriots that marched on Washington, D.C., on September 12, 2009.

Copywrited by B. Leland Baker on 09/12/09

CHAPTER 1

The Conscience Defined

What is a conservative? This seems like a simple question, but I discovered that many self-described conservatives do not know or understand the definition. Participating in many town-hall meetings and political chat rooms reinforced my findings that many conservatives often define themselves by their membership or alignment with the Republican Party. Similarly, many self-described liberals define themselves by their membership or alignment with the Democrat Party.

While the "Conservative equals Republican" and "Liberal equals Democrat" equations might have been true at some time in the past, they are no longer true today. The propagandists from both major political parties have brainwashed the party loyalists into believing that up is down, left is right, and that tax means invest. Party elites and their propagandists have taught their followers that "Big Government" Republican programs are conservative, but "Big Government" Democrat programs are liberal. Tea Partiers know that both are wrong.

As predicted by Barry Goldwater in 1964, the two major parties have become one corrupt entity. There are a handful of social viewpoints that are used by party propagandists to stir up people's emotions, but nothing of significance differentiates the harm done to the American people by the Republican or Democrat progressive political elites. Tea Partiers are citizens who have learned to focus on the *behavior* of their elected officials, not their *words.*

Like Thomas Jefferson and Barry Goldwater, Tea Partiers have five foundational beliefs that are interconnected:

- Constitutional compliance
- Smaller federal government
- States' rights
- Lower spending and taxes
- Individual rights, responsibility, and integrity

The following paragraphs will give a brief overview of these concepts.

I. Constitutional Compliance

What do Tea Partiers mean by "Constitutional Compliance"?

Thomas Jefferson wrote that the United States Constitution is necessarily a restrictive, not a permissive, document. It describes the powers of the U.S. federal government and provides an amendment process for changing those powers. The Bill of Rights lists freedoms of our people that should not be violated by the political elites and power brokers in Washington, D.C.

Our Founding Fathers looked upon the federal role as limited government. Why? Because history has proven that the more power a government takes from its citizens, the less freedom those citizens enjoy. This was true during the Roman Empire, the monarchies of the Middle Ages, and the many dictatorships of the twentieth century.

II. Smaller Federal Government

If our politicians adhered to the powers granted in the U.S. Constitution, then the size of the federal government would be substantially smaller. For example, many entities such as the Department of Education would not exist. This will be explained in greater detail in subsequent chapters. Tea Partiers are *not* anarchists; we are merely opposed to excessive growth in government that is *not* authorized by the United States Constitution.

III. States' Rights

Our 10th Amendment states, "The powers *not* delegated to the United States by the Constitution, nor prohibited by it to the States, are reserved to the States respectively, or to the people." In plain English, this means that if a very specific power is not stated in the U.S. Constitution, then our states or people retain that power. This is an important axiom that reinforces the Tea Party plank against an enlarged U.S. federal government.

IV. Lower Spending and Taxes

If the U.S. government were smaller, then federal spending would be smaller, and fewer unnecessary taxes would be confiscated from our paychecks. The federal and state tax systems in the United States are intended to serve separate functions and distinct jurisdictions. But the federal government has encroached upon state and local roles as well. The 16th Amendment to the Constitution initiated the U.S. income tax in 1913.

Congress promptly passed a new income tax law with rates beginning at 1 percent and rising to 7 percent for taxpayers with higher income; however, less than 1 percent of the population paid income tax at that time. Today, many of us lose almost a third of our wages to an insatiable federal appetite.

V. Individual Rights, Responsibility, and Integrity

There was a time when individual responsibility and integrity did not need to be explained. However, we now live in a society ruled by a legal system which makes excuses for convicted murderers (e.g., he had a "bad childhood") or for groups of individuals (resulting in unconstitutional discrimination). This "victimology" mentality allows the federal government to act as a monarch saving her serfs.

Integrity is inseparable from individual responsibility. Our elected officials often don't get it. For instance, Article II, Section 4, of the Constitution states: "the President, Vice President, and all civil officers of the United States shall be removed from office on impeachment for, and conviction of, treason, bribery, or other high crimes and misdemeanors." E.g., Mr. Wm. Clinton was impeached for perjury related to sexual misconduct. Perjury is a felony, yet he was not removed. Why should laws against perjury apply to you and me, but *not* our elected officials?

Tea Partiers do not believe in a class-based or caste-based society where elected officials are allowed to lie, cheat, or steal, but common citizens are prosecuted for similar conduct. As per Title 18, U.S. Code Section 1621, a citizen could face up to five years in jail for lying under oath. The Democrat political elites' support for Clinton after his felonious perjury in 1998 shows their loyalty to "party" rather than equality before the law, ensuring fairness to all American citizens.

Throughout this text, I do not routinely use titles such as president, senator, or congressman when referring to *former* elected officials. This is intentional because Tea Partiers understand that these elected officials are in *temporary* positions to <u>serve</u> the people, not vice versa. In a republic or democracy, the concept of a monarch, king, president, or "official" for life is repugnant.

Americans who are <u>loyal</u> to our constitutional principles should insist that upon leaving public office, the former elected official should stop using his or her former title. To do otherwise is to return to the monarch-serf mentality that existed before we threw off the yoke of English aristocracy.

> *Tea Partiers support the U.S. Constitution because it empowers the government to maintain social order, while simultaneously guaranteeing individual freedom.*

CHAPTER 2

Perils of Absolute Power

Tea Partiers know that the highest law of the land is the United States Constitution. It defines the legitimate functions of the three branches of the federal government. If the function is listed, then it is legitimate, but if a function or power is not listed, then it is not legitimate. Strictly adhering to functions and powers as listed in the U.S. Constitution without expansive interpretation keeps the federal government from growing too large and abusive.

The intent of dividing the key functions of the federal government among three separate, but equal, branches is to keep the United States from becoming a monarchy, dictatorship, or totalitarian state.

Article 1 explains the legislative process and power to pass laws vested in the U.S. Congress, which consists of the House of Representatives and the Senate.

Article 2 describes the executive power that is vested in our president; and it further designates the U.S. president as the commander in chief of the Army and

Navy of the United States.

Article 3 vests the judicial power in one Supreme Court and in such inferior courts as the Congress may, from time to time, ordain and establish.

The amendment process that is described in the Constitution provides a means for modifying federal powers, while protecting our states and citizens. Article 5 describes these procedures, which include ratification by the legislatures of three-fourths of the several states.

Why do checks and balances matter?

The checks and balances *should* matter because they prevent one branch or one person from taking absolute power. Historical examples can be found where kings with absolute power executed serfs for minor infractions. In the last century, dictators in Nazi Germany and Communist Russia executed millions of their own citizens without cause. Leaders of totalitarian regimes throughout history have abused power—and the common man has suffered.

> *Power tends to corrupt and absolute power corrupts absolutely.* —Lord Acton

When did the U.S. checks and balances stop working?

In 1788, James Madison identified that "there are more instances of the abridgement of freedom of the people by gradual and silent encroachments of those in power than by violent and sudden usurpations." There is not a specific date that U.S. constitutional checks and balances stopped working, because our elected officials began ignoring the Constitution *incrementally*. If our political elites attempted revolutionary change, then people would have noticed— and fought back. So, our elected officials implemented incremental changes that were often not noticed by the public.

For example, our Constitution requires the president to swear this oath before assuming office:

> *"I do solemnly swear (or affirm) that I will faithfully execute the Office of President of the United States, and will to the best of my ability, preserve, protect and defend the Constitution of the United States."*

Despite this oath, most of our presidents have violated the Constitution; so, too, have members of the Congress and the Supreme Court. The checks and balances are not working! For example, the Department of Education (ED) was created by the U.S. Congress and signed into law by Mr. Jimmy Carter on October 17, 1979 (Public Law 96– 88); ED began operating on May 4, 1980.

The Congress created a cabinet post even though *education* is not a specified role in the U.S. Constitution

The former president signed it into law in violation of his oath to preserve, protect, and defend the Constitution

The Supreme Court either looked the other way or claimed that the "commerce clause" covered everything, and barred nothing

The governors of the various states *should* have protested, but they didn't

Tea Partiers view the U.S. Constitution as a moral and legal mandate that ensures the concept of a limited federal government. The Constitution is a contract between the governed and governing. The creation of the Department of Education is one of hundreds of examples that show an incremental deviation from and disregard for the Constitution by elected officials.

Did the Republicans do this? Did the Democrats do this? Elected officials from *both* major parties are guilty of numerous violations of constitutionally designated powers.

Tea Partiers recognize that a large part of the problems we face today is that many of our elected officials in all three branches of government have greater loyalty to their political party than they do to the highest law of the land or to their constituents.

> *Tea Partiers recognize that the separation of powers and the constitutional amendment process are being ignored by our political elites and we're fed up!*

CHAPTER **3**

States' Rights

Tea Partiers understand that federal adherence to the U.S. Constitution is important for every state and every individual. This stems from an understanding of human nature:

- Parents have influence with children in a family
- The neighborhood association is influenced by families and homeowners
- The small-town or city mayor is normally responsive to local citizens, families, and homeowners
- The county government is normally more distant than the town or city officials and may be *slightly* less responsive
- The state government is normally less responsive than town, city, or county, but is responsive to state issues
- The federal government is the most removed from the issues of one's neighborhood, and should, therefore, have the least amount of power

No Commitment

Neither the Republican nor Democrat political elites maintain a meaningful commitment to states' rights, even though the U.S. Constitution establishes a distinction between federal and state jurisdiction.

Federal aid to states, organizations, or individuals comes out of taxpayer pockets, and a percentage is retained by the federal government as overhead. The remainder is gifted to the federal beneficiary. This federal overhead "tax" could be as small as 10 percent or as high as 50 percent.

This was demonstrated by the recent "bail-out" money and reckless spending by the federal government during the last year of the Bush administration and the first year of the Obama administration. A majority of federal grants or matching funds are in areas that belong to the states.

- Why does the federal government provide scholarships, grants, or any funding to state colleges and universities?
- Why does the federal government provide monies to any of the various states or private entities?

These are not specified roles in the U.S. Constitution. In addition, the United States government does not produce revenue, but obtains funds through taxation or printing. Since the federal government is involved in many areas not permitted by the Constitution, our taxation is too high.

Governors

Our governors should jealously guard states' rights from federal intrusion and encroachment. Most of them do not! State governors, who are addicted to federal handouts, are the equivalent of individuals addicted to cocaine. It is hard to stop using, once started.

Much has been written on how Franklin D. Roosevelt influenced elections through the use of federal funds during the New Deal. Similarly, Lyndon B. Johnson successfully replicated the same unconstitutional playbook supporting the Great Society in functions that belong to the states. Johnson's War on Poverty

- Initiated community-based antipoverty programs
- Provided significant federal aid to public education
- Initiated "socialized medicine" through Medicare to everyone over 65
- Initiated "free health care" for the poor through Medicaid (Tea Partiers know *nothing* is free)

Superficially, all of these programs were kindhearted and compassionate, but they are not constitutional functions of the federal government and are, therefore, illegal confiscation and redistribution of our wealth. Our Republican and Democrat elected officials have been too lazy to initiate the amendment process as mandated by the Constitution. In addition, our state governors have not protested the takeover of these state functions by the federal government. State governors have permitted themselves to be marginalized by suckling the federal government's monetary-tit.

Today, as a result of political elites who manipulate propaganda, combined with decades of apathy or inattention, the Bush and Obama administrations' handouts and bailouts to state entities and private organizations are perceived as a *normal* way of doing business in Washington, D.C.

Tea Partiers intuitively know this is unconstitutional, which has given rise to our Tea Party movement.

Retaking State Authority

Governors should lead the charge in retaking states' rights, power, and authority from the federal government. The following are examples of encroachments on states' rights:

- The Department of Health and Human Services (HHS). Created in 1953, HHS is the United States government's principal agency for protecting the health of all Americans and providing essential human services, especially for those who are least able to help themselves. The work of HHS is conducted by the Office of the Secretary and 11 agencies that perform a wide variety of tasks and services, including research, public health, food and drug safety, grants and other funding, health insurance, and many others. In addition, HHS administers Medicare and Medicaid, which (allegedly) provide health insurance to one in four Americans. http://www.hhs.gov

» Issues: Health care is *not* a function enumerated in the U.S. Constitution; hence, the HHS "redistributes wealth" through the Medicare and Medicaid programs, functions not enumerated in the U.S. Constitution.

» Solution: Pass an amendment to the Constitution or eliminate HHS for a cost savings of over $700 billion.

- **The Department of Education** (ED) Created in 1980, ED establishes policies on federal financial aid for education, and distributes as well as monitors those funds; collects data on America's schools and disseminates research. http://www.ed.gov

  » Issues: None of these functions are enumerated in the U.S. Constitution, yet Mr. Bush claimed to be the "Education President." Bizarre!

  » Solution: Pass an amendment to the Constitution or eliminate ED for a cost savings of over $68 billion.

- **The Department of Energy** (DOE). Created in 1977, the DOE Web site identifies its roles as increasing energy supplies, modernizing our energy infrastructure, ensuring the productive and optimal use of energy resources, while limiting environmental impact and cooperating on international energy issues. DOE is also tasked with ensuring America's nuclear security. www.Energy.gov

» Issues: Energy is not a function enumerated in the U.S. Constitution. In addition, the DOE "redistributes" wealth through grants to state energy programs.

» Solution: Pass an amendment to the Constitution or eliminate DOE for a cost savings of over $23 billion.

- **The Department of Housing and Urban Development (HUD)** HUD's mission is to increase home ownership, support community development, and increase access to affordable housing free from discrimination. To fulfill this mission, HUD will embrace high standards of ethics, management, and accountability and forge new partnerships—particularly with faith-based and community organizations—that leverage resources and improve HUD's ability to be effective on the community level. www.HUD.gov

» Issues: Housing is not a function enumerated in the U.S. Constitution. In addition, the HUD "redistributes" wealth through grants and public housing programs. Despite major failures in government-run housing, it still continues as a drain on our revenues.

» Solution: Pass an amendment to the Constitution or eliminate HUD for a cost savings of over $40 billion.

- **Department of Transportation (DOT)** DOT's mission is to serve the United States by ensuring a fast, safe, efficient, accessible, and convenient transportation system that meets our vital national interests and enhances the quality of life of the American people, today and into the future. Organizations within the DOT include the Federal Aviation Administration, the National Highway Traffic Safety Administration, and the Maritime Administration. www.DOT.gov

  » Issues: Transportation is not a function enumerated in the U.S. Constitution. In addition, the DOT "redistributes" wealth through state and local grants and other transportation programs.

  » Solution: Pass an amendment to the Constitution to clarify, through debate, whether *anything* in the DOT mission falls under the commerce clause of the Constitution or eliminate DOT for a cost savings of over $70 billion.

- **The Department of Agriculture (USDA)** USDA provides leadership on food, agriculture, natural resources, and related issues based on sound public policy, the best available science, and efficient management. www.usda.gov

  » Issues: No power over agriculture was given to any branch of the national government by the Constitution.

Solution: Initiate an amendment to the Constitution or eliminate USDA for a cost savings of over $95 billion.

- **Department of Labor (DOL)** The DOL's mission is to foster and promote the welfare of job seekers, wage earners, and retirees of the United States by improving their working conditions, advancing their opportunities for profitable employment, protecting their retirement and health-care benefits, helping employers find workers, strengthening free collective bargaining, and tracking changes in employment, prices, and other national economic measurements. www.DOL.gov

  » Issues: Job training, working conditions, minimum hourly wages, overtime pay, and unemployment insurance are not functions enumerated in the U.S. Constitution; and, therefore, should be retained by the states. DOL "redistributes" wealth through grants, the Job Corps, and other programs. Tea Partiers favor states' "right-to-work laws" that eliminates union membership as a condition of employment. Unions serve a purpose, but joining should be voluntary, not mandatory.

  » Solution: Initiate an amendment to the Constitution to clarify, through debate, whether the DOL mission falls under the commerce clause of the U.S. Constitution or eliminate DOL for a cost savings of over $60 billion.

- The Federal Emergency Management Agency, or FEMA, was initially created by Presidential Order on April 1, 1979. On March 1, 2003, FEMA became part of the U.S. Department of Homeland Security (DHS). FEMA's primary mission is to reduce the loss of life and property and protect the nation from all hazards. www.fema.gov

  » Issues: Creating FEMA by Presidential Order encroaches upon the Congress's legislative powers. All-hazards protection was the responsibility of states, and without an amendment, it still is. FEMA "redistributes" wealth after natural or other disasters.

  » Solution: Initiate an amendment to the Constitution to clarify, through debate, whether the FEMA mission should be included in the Constitution or eliminate FEMA for a cost savings of over $6 billion.

Spending on these programs, which were never authorized through the Constitution's amendment process, is as shown in this chart:

Spending by Departments that were not created by Constitutional Amendment

	USDA	ED	DOE	HHS	HUD	DOL	DOT
1964	7.6	1.0	2.7	4.6	0.1	3.5	4.7
1965	6.9	1.2	2.6	4.7	0.5	3.1	5.2
1966	5.6	2.4	2.3	5.7	2.5	3.2	5.1
1967	6.0	3.6	2.3	9.6	3.1	3.6	5.2
1968	7.4	4.1	2.5	13.1	3.7	4.2	5.6
1969	8.4	4.0	2.4	15.4	0.7	4.2	5.7
1970	8.4	4.6	2.4	17.4	2.4	5.0	6.1
1971	8.7	5.1	2.2	20.4	2.8	8.5	7.0
1972	11.0	5.5	2.3	25.3	3.6	10.4	7.2
1973	10.2	5.7	2.3	25.6	3.6	9.6	7.8
1974	10.3	5.7	2.2	28.1	4.8	10.0	7.7
1975	15.5	7.3	3.2	33.8	7.5	18.6	9.1
1976	17.7	7.9	3.8	40.3	7.0	26.5	11.7
TQ	5.0	2.0	1.0	10.5	1.4	6.1	2.9
1977	23.3	8.7	5.0	46.5	5.8	23.2	12.0
1978	30.2	9.8	6.4	51.8	7.7	23.7	12.8
1979	31.7	12.2	7.4	57.8	9.2	23.4	14.6
1980	34.7	14.6	7.3	68.3	12.7	30.5	18.2
1981	41.5	17.0	11.8	80.8	14.9	30.9	20.9
1982	45.6	14.7	11.7	88.4	15.2	31.5	17.9
1983	52.3	14.4	10.6	95.0	15.8	38.7	18.2
1984	41.9	15.4	11.0	102.4	16.7	25.3	20.5
1985	55.4	16.6	10.6	114.3	28.7	24.7	22.5
1986	58.6	17.6	11.0	122.9	14.1	24.9	24.9
1987	49.5	16.7	10.7	131.4	15.5	24.2	22.9
1988	43.9	18.1	11.2	140.0	18.9	22.7	23.7
1989	48.3	21.5	11.4	152.7	19.7	23.4	23.8
1990	45.9	23.0	12.1	175.5	20.2	26.1	25.6
1991	54.0	25.2	12.5	198.1	22.8	34.8	27.2
1992	56.3	25.8	15.5	231.6	24.5	47.9	29.1
1993	63.0	30.1	16.9	253.8	25.2	45.5	31.0
1994	60.6	24.6	17.8	278.9	25.8	37.8	33.6
1995	56.6	31.2	17.6	303.1	29.0	32.8	35.1
1996	54.2	29.7	16.2	319.8	25.2	33.2	35.1
1997	52.4	30.0	14.5	339.5	27.5	31.1	36.1
1998	53.8	31.5	14.4	350.6	30.2	30.6	35.6
1999	62.7	31.3	15.9	359.7	32.7	33.0	37.7
2000	75.5	33.9	15.0	382.6	30.8	31.9	41.5
2001	68.0	35.7	16.3	426.3	33.9	39.8	49.3
2002	68.7	46.3	17.7	465.8	31.9	64.7	56.0
2003	72.4	57.4	19.4	505.3	37.5	69.6	50.8
2004	71.8	62.8	20.0	543.4	45.0	56.7	54.5
2005	94.9	71.0	22.2	585.8	42.6	50.0	58.2
2006	94.6	64.3	22.0	643.9	40.2	51.7	60.6
2007	90.8	61.9	21.4	694.0	37.1	48.3	60.7
2008	88.9	60.7	20.2	735.2	33.4	50.4	61.5
2009	87.7	60.3	19.4	780.8	31.4	53.1	64.6
Subtotals	$ 2,059	$ 1,094	$ 507	$ 10,080	$ 866	$ 1,333	$ 1,228

Total Unconstitutional spending = over $17 Trillion

The Amendment Process and State Rights

Creation of cabinet posts and massive federal agencies with multibillion dollar budgets should be debated and approved or disapproved according to the processes in Article 5 of the U.S. Constitution. As one can see from the chart, total spending by the departments that were not constitutionally authorized through our amendment process equals more than $17 trillion since 1964. This would be enough to retire the current federal debt.

If functions such as health, housing, education, energy, transportation, labor, agriculture, and emergency management are better conducted at the federal level, then these functions will survive the amendment process, to include ratification by the legislatures of three-fourths of the states.

If these functions do not survive the amendment process, then the departments or agencies must be closed and their programs must be eliminated. The federal government must eliminate all programs that are not constitutionally mandated or American citizens will see the collapse of our economy and the devaluation of the of the American dollar.

Our elected federal officials want the federal government to have a great deal of power over the entire economy, the states, and individuals' behavior. It's all about control.

CHAPTER 4

Individual Rights, Responsibilities, and Integrity

The Bill of Rights, the first 10 amendments to the U.S. Constitution, lists our individual rights and freedoms as envisioned by our Founding Fathers. This short summary is not all inclusive:

- Freedom to practice religious beliefs
- Freedom from a state-mandated religion
- Free speech & press
- Peaceful assembly
- Petition the government
- Own a weapon
- Freedom from soldiers living in your home
- No unreasonable searches and seizures
- Not testifying against yourself
- Not deprived of life, liberty, or property without due process of law (a trial)
- Property not confiscated without just compensation
- Speedy trial with an impartial jury, counsel, and

witnesses for defense
- Trial by jury for lawsuits greater than $20
- No excessive bail or fines
- No cruel or unusual punishments
- Rights belong to either the states or the people if not enumerated for the federal government

> *Incrementally, many of these rights have been violated or ignored by our elected officials & the political elites*

As discussed in previous chapters, the rights or powers that are not specifically delegated to the federal government belong to either the states or the people. The discussion of federal encroachment upon state functions is similar to the encroachment upon citizens' civil liberties.

Conscription

One of the liberties that many Americans take for granted is the freedom to live our lives as we choose. The most egregious violation of America's freedom was the military conscription, or "draft," during the Viet Nam conflict. Tea Partiers will always support and defend the Constitution, so a draft will never be needed to raise a militia or military force to protect American borders. However, the Viet Nam conflict was yet another example of federal incrementalism. The U.S. Congress did not declare war against a sovereign nation since North Viet Nam did not pose a direct threat to the United States. Instead, the president conducted an undeclared and unconstitutional war by incrementally increasing the number of soldiers involved in the conflict.

Since the military had difficulty achieving enlistment goals, conscription was relied upon to meet recruitment goals.

In the 1960s, party elites defined patriotism as support for the Viet Nam war and the draft. Forcing people into military service against their wills violates the constitutional prohibition of involuntary servitude; but military conscription continued under both Democrat and Republican administrations. In addition, both parties permitted the president of the United States to conduct a war without a formal declaration of war as mandated in the United States Constitution. So, not only were we fighting an unconstitutional conflict, but our nation was creating involuntary indentured servants to fight it.

This is relevant today because the U.S. Congress has discussed conscription to support the wars in Iraq and Afghanistan. Tea Partiers understand that your life belongs to you, not civil servants in a faceless federal bureaucracy.

> *The draft rests on the assumption that your kids belong to the state . . . The Nazis thought it was a great idea.*
> — Ronald Reagan (1979)

Civil Forfeiture

Many Americans take our "right to own property" for granted, but "civil forfeiture" laws permit confiscation of our property. Using the War on Drugs and more recently, the War on Terror, the federal government has established laws and procedures to seize the property of individuals *without* going through the due process guaranteed by our Constitution.

In U.S. legal tradition, the burden of proof is upon

the government prosecutors, whereas, in civil forfeiture, the "claimant shall have the burden of proving that the claimant is an innocent owner by a preponderance of the evidence." Hence, Title 18 U.S. Code, Section 983 and Title 21 U.S. Code, Section 981 violate the due process clause of the Constitution.

Eminent Domain

The U.S. Supreme Court has held that the federal government and each state have the power of eminent domain, which is the power to take away our private property for "public use." The Takings Clause, the last clause of the Fifth Amendment, states that property shall not be taken for public use without just compensation. Abuses of eminent domain have resulted in nationwide grassroots property rights projects, such as the Institute for Justice's Castle Coalition. The Institute teaches home and business owners how to protect themselves and stand up to the greedy government officials and developers who seek to use eminent domain to take private property for their own profit. http://www.ij.org/

Unreasonable Searches and Seizures

The Uniting and Strengthening America by Providing Appropriate Tools Required to Intercept and Obstruct Terrorism Act of 2001, abbreviated as the USA PATRIOT Act, was passed with virtually no debate. Few, if any, of our congressmen actually read the bill before the vote, yet it was passed by wide margins in Congress. It was supported by members of both the Republican and Democratic parties, further demonstrating collusion between the political elites of the two majority parties.

Tea Partiers are concerned about compliance with the Constitution and potential abuses of any of our freedoms. Hence, the USA PATRIOT Act has been the subject of discussion by Tea Partiers and civil libertarians alike. Elements of the USA PATRIOT Act threaten our constitutional freedoms by giving the government the power to access and seize medical records, tax records, information about the books you buy or borrow, and lists of individuals who belong to political organizations *without probable cause.* The Act also authorizes government officials to break into your home and conduct secret "sneak-and-peek" searches without a constitutionally mandated warrant that describes the place to be searched and the persons or things to be seized.

If you think it is "creepy" that your home can be searched without a warrant or any other notification, you are a normal American citizen; if you recognize this as an abuse of constitutional power, then you are most likely a liberty-loving Tea Partier.

> ***Resistance to tyrants is obedience to God.***
> —Thomas Jefferson

Violating Due Process

Another example of governmental abuse focuses upon Jose Padilla, who was suspected of being associated with al-Qaeda and planning terrorist attacks in the United States. The executive branch of the Bush administration arrested this American citizen without charging him with a crime; held him in a naval brig in South Carolina for two years; denied him access to a lawyer; and prohibited any contact with his friends and family.

Tea Partiers recognize that whether the accused is guilty or not, due process mandates that a citizen cannot be detained indefinitely without being charged with a crime, he should be given legal counsel, and he should be provided a fair trial. The Second Circuit Court agreed, writing that "the President does not have the power under Article II of the Constitution to detain as an enemy combatant an American citizen seized on American soil outside a zone of combat."

Gun Rights

The Second Amendment guarantees the right to bear arms. Tea Partiers understand that U.S. citizens not only have the right to buy a gun, but also have the responsibility to learn the proper operation and maintenance of their weapons. We recognize that lawful gun ownership reduces violent crime when accompanied by laws that support gun-owners' rights over those of lawbreakers.

> *The strongest reason for the people to retain the right to keep and bear arms is, as a last resort, to protect themselves against tyranny in government.*
> —Thomas Jefferson

If our elected officials supported and defended the Constitution in its entirety, then organizations such as the National Rifle Association would be unnecessary. However, full government control of the economy cannot be accomplished if citizens own firearms; therefore, gun rights have continuously remained under assault by party elites, and patriots like Mr. Rick Stanley have been jailed. http://victimsoflaw.net/Stanley.htm.

No Federal Authority

While ignoring violations of rights that are guaranteed by the U.S. Constitution, many of our political elites and federally elected officials talk about the federal government fulfilling the "right" to free health care, the "right" to a welfare check, the "right" to education, or the "right" to housing with a low interest mortgage. Tea Partiers see this rhetoric for what it is: propaganda by elected officials and handouts to buy votes.

Tea Partiers understand that if a function has not been added to the Constitution through the amendment process, then it is not a federal authority. You have the right to purchase or not purchase health insurance, but the federal government does not have the constitutional authority to provide it to you. Yet, our elected officials continue talking about rights and federal authorities that do not exist. Many continue to violate or ignore the fundamental rights that are guaranteed by the U.S. Constitution and our Bill of Rights.

Responsibility and Integrity

Tea Partiers understand that with rights come both responsibility and integrity. Citizens have the responsibility to analyze candidates' stances on campaign issues and vote for candidates who will "preserve, protect, and defend *the Constitution."* Many citizens vote for their favorite singing stars on *American Idol* but do not vote in national elections. They then complain vociferously when the government takes another percentage of taxes from their paychecks. Tea Parties are evidence that this is starting to change.

Tea Partiers understand the interrelationship between rights, responsibility, and integrity. Without honesty and adherence to moral and ethical principles, our elected officials cannot be trusted. Very simply, Tea Partiers expect our elected officials to comply with the Constitution and not to cheat, lie, steal, murder, or commit adultery.

Is that too much to ask?

One of the better examples of government self-policing is our military, because they punish service members who lie, steal, murder, commit adultery, or conduct other crimes. Although the military is not crime-free, it is great to know that a soldier, sailor, airman, or marine's word still counts. Unfortunately, our elected officials are not routinely held to the same level of integrity and standards of conduct as a private in the U.S. military.

> *Nobody can acquire honor by doing what is wrong.*
> – Thomas Jefferson

CHAPTER 5

Economics, Taxes, and Spending

What Are the Economic "-isms"?

When one discusses economics, there are three primary "isms" to include: capitalism, socialism, and communism.

- **Capitalism** is focused upon individual production and private control of the economy; redistribution of wealth is voluntary through charitable organizations.
- **Socialism** is governmental ownership and administration of the means of production and forced redistribution of wealth or goods in the name of fairness (Progressives are American Socialists who advocate Big Government programs—higher spending & taxes).
- **Communism** has historically been an extreme form of socialism, often combined with violent implementation.

Excluding Cuba and North Korea, most economies have varying degrees of both capitalism and socialism. Most industrialized and developed economies may have a mixture of state-control and private-control of their means of production. Philosophically, Big Government Socialists and Progressives use the phrase coined by Karl Marx:

> *"From each according to his abilities, to each according to his needs"* —Karl Marx (1875)

Socialism, or progressivism, is the path that has been followed by both Republican and Democrat political elites for the past 80 years (political elites, not necessarily the general membership). Our elected officials in the White House, the Congress, and the courts have either embraced or ignored this unconstitutional shift of power as articulated in previous chapters. The political elites have stepped up their propaganda campaigns against anyone who opposes their goals for greater centralized control, labeling opponents as either: mean-spirited, racist, or anti-family. It's the economy stupid! Tea Partiers understand this is merely to deflect attention from an unconstitutional and illegal takeover of the economy.

Economically, Republican and Democrat political elites have become Socialistic-Progressives, who want government to have a great deal of power over the economy, who doubt whether economic liberty and individual freedom are practical options in today's world. They tend to distrust the free market, support high taxes, and centralized planning of the economy.

Long before the massive federal bailouts and handouts by the Bush and Obama administrations, the United

States was on a slippery slope to a government-controlled economy. An obvious example includes the Medicare and Medicaid health insurance programs that were *never* authorized through a constitutional amendment.

Similarly, George W. Bush went into office under the guise of being a conservative. Yet, during Bush's tenure, he embraced a prescription drug program that has already cost taxpayers billions, and might cost as much as $1 trillion in its first decade. Beware of wolves in sheep's clothing! This is a routine example of Big Government taking from the workforce according to their abilities and giving to the prescription beneficiaries according to their perceived needs. How very progressive of you, Mr. Bush!

Tea Partiers know that prescription drug benefits are *not* enumerated in the Constitution. Bush often spoke as a conservative, but acted like a socialistic-progressive. Political doublespeak also goes back to Tea Partiers' values and belief in integrity: we believe our elected officials should say what they mean, and mean what they say. Most often, they don't.

Tea Partiers believe in the limitations on federal power as articulated in the Constitution because those limits make the federal government's size and functions smaller. If the U.S. government is smaller, then fewer taxes are needed. If fewer taxes are confiscated, then individuals have greater liberty to spend as they choose. The federal government *should not* have an unlimited claim on the earnings of its citizens.

- Tea Partiers believe that citizens can spend our wages and earnings better than the government!
- Socialists or Progressives believe that the government

can spend our earnings better than we can!

Tea Partiers believe that individual motivation and hard work results in success for the individual and his or her family. Socialistic-Progressives believe the government is obligated to *level the playing field* so that all citizens have a "fair" life, without regard to individual motivation or hard work. This attitude toward fairness results in federal confiscation of wealth from taxpayers and redistribution of wealth to other individuals or groups who did not earn it.

The question asked by all taxpayers include: "How much is enough?" But Tea Partiers ask, "How can we maintain our liberty and freedom if our income or wealth is confiscated?" And "enough" is defined by the U.S. Constitution. If citizens are taxed to meet the specified functions listed in the Constitution, then *that* is enough. If our taxes support the world of good ideas not specified in the Constitution, then that is too much.

Tea Partiers believe that taxes should be high enough to maintain law and order (rate of 10 percent or less), whereas Big Government Socialists and Progressives do not believe that confiscating <u>half</u> of your income is unreasonable!

Fiscal Irresponsibility

The primary problem that Americans face is that our elected officials have become irresponsible, without consequences imposed upon them. The checks and balances have not kept our elected officials from overspending and placing our children and grandchildren in fiscal bondage for the next century. The federal government created serfs without firing a shot.

A review of the charts below reveal decades of fiscal irresponsibility, whether the White House was occupied by a Republican or Democrat, and without regard to who had a majority in Congress.

RECEIPTS, OUTLAYS, & SURPLUSES OR DEFICITS

	Year	Total (millions)		
		Receipts	Outlays	Surplus or Deficit(−)
Mr. Johnson	1964	112,613	118,528	-5,915
	1965	116,817	118,228	-1,411
	1966	130,835	134,532	-3,698
	1967	148,822	157,464	-8,643
	1968	152,973	178,134	-25,161
Mr. Nixon	1969	186,882	183,640	3,242
	1970	192,807	195,649	-2,842
	1971	187,139	210,172	-23,033
	1972	207,309	230,681	-23,373
	1973	230,799	245,707	-14,908
Mr. Ford	1974	263,224	269,359	-6,135
	1975	279,090	332,332	-53,242
	1976	298,060	371,792	-73,732
	TQ	81,232	95,975	-14,744
Mr. Carter	1977	355,559	409,218	-53,659
	1978	399,561	458,746	-59,185
	1979	463,302	504,028	-40,726
	1980	517,112	590,941	-73,830
Mr. Reagan	1981	599,272	678,241	-78,968
	1982	617,766	745,743	-127,977
	1983	600,562	808,364	-207,802
	1984	666,486	851,853	-185,367
	1985	734,088	946,396	-212,308
	1986	769,215	990,441	-221,227
	1987	854,353	1,004,083	-149,730
	1988	909,303	1,064,481	-155,178

RECEIPTS, OUTLAYS, & SURPLUSES OR DEFICITS

	Year	Total (millions)		
		Receipts	Outlays	Surplus or Deficit(−)
Mr. Bush	1989	991,190	1,143,829	-152,639
	1990	1,032,094	1,253,130	-221,036
	1991	1,055,093	1,324,331	-269,238
	1992	1,091,328	1,381,649	-290,321
Mr. Clinton	1993	1,154,471	1,409,522	-255,051
	1994	1,258,721	1,461,907	-203,186
	1995	1,351,932	1,515,884	-163,952
	1996	1,453,177	1,560,608	-107,431
	1997	1,579,423	1,601,307	-21,884
	1998	1,721,955	1,652,685	69,270
	1999	1,827,645	1,702,035	125,610
	2000	2,025,457	1,789,216	236,241
Mr. Bush	2001	1,991,426	1,863,190	128,236
	2002	1,853,395	2,011,153	-157,758
	2003	1,782,532	2,160,117	-377,585
	2004	1,880,279	2,293,006	-412,727
	2005	2,153,859	2,472,205	-318,346
	2006	2,407,254	2,655,435	-248,181
	2007	2,568,239	2,728,940	-160,701
	2008	2,524,326	2,982,881	-458,555
Mr. Obama	2009 est	2,156,654	3,997,842	-1,841,188

http://www.whitehouse.gov/omb/budget/Historicals/

Tea Partiers believe that our property, wealth, and freedom are inseparable. Confiscation of lives, property, or wealth is an attack on our freedom. America was founded upon an understanding that our citizens have the right to the possession and use of their property and earnings. But, Americans have been under attack since the 1913 creation of the federal income tax by a federal government that no longer follows the rule of law. This chart shows that an appetite for federal governmental growth is accompanied by fiscal irresponsibility with billion-dollar deficits mounting into an ever-increasing 14 trillion-dollar debt.

Boiled American Frogs

Allegedly, if you drop a live frog into a pot of hot water, it will try to jump out of the water; but if you put the frog into warm water and gradually increase the temperature, it will remain there and be boiled. American citizens are similar to the frog; we have been boiled by our elected officials. If the income tax enacted in 1913 was based upon a confiscation of 33 percent of our income, then Americans would have rioted in the streets of every major city. U.S. congressmen would have been hung from tall trees with short ropes for enacting that legislation; and the president would, most likely, have been tarred and feathered. American frogs would have jumped into action! However, the political elites in both parties grew the federal government and increased taxation incrementally. The Federal Tax Rates began at 1 percent in 1913 and have risen to the point where most middle-class Americans are working about one-third of their lives for the government.

Tax Freedom Day

The Tax Foundation calculates "tax freedom day" each year and has determined that our income is consumed by taxes from January 1 to April 13 this year. If we include the current deficit in these calculations, then tax freedom day did not occur until May 29, 2009. (www.taxfoundation. org)

Tea Partiers are disgusted by the reckless spending of the Bush and Obama administrations. It is not necessary, and is not in the interests of the American people. How can any individual or family get ahead if four or five months of earnings are confiscated by the federal government and then gifted to people who did not earn it?

This table and chart show the explosion in irresponsible federal spending since the creation of the Great Society. Federal debt has grown exponentially from $311 billion in 1964 to over $14 trillion in 2009. In addition, due to reckless spending by Big Government politicians in the Bush and Obama administrations, the debt to GDP ratio has exceeded 90 percent, resulting in a country that is on the brink of fiscal collapse.

Fiscal Year	Gross Debt	GDP	Debt/GDP	Fiscal Year	Gross Debt	GDP	Debt/GDP
Johnson '64	316	641	49%	Bush '89	2,868	5,401	53%
	322	687	47%		3,206	5,736	56%
	328	755	44%		3,598	5,938	61%
	340	811	42%		4,002	6,243	64%
	369	867	43%	Clinton '93	4,351	6,583	66%
Nixon '69	366	948	39%		4,643	6,961	67%
	381	1,013	38%		4,921	7,322	67%
	408	1,080	38%		5,181	7,699	67%
	436	1,178	37%		5,369	8,185	66%
	466	1,310	36%		5,478	8,627	64%
Ford '74	484	1,440	34%		5,606	9,130	61%
	542	1,562	35%		5,629	9,705	58%
	629	1,737	36%	Bush '01	5,770	10,052	57%
	644	1,839	35%		6,198	10,383	60%
Carter '77	706	1,973	36%		6,760	10,799	63%
	777	2,219	35%		7,355	11,510	64%
	829	2,506	33%		7,905	12,237	65%
	909	2,722	33%		8,451	13,002	65%
Reagan '81	995	3,061	33%		8,951	13,644	66%
	1,137	3,222	35%		9,986	14,225	70%
	1,372	3,446	40%	Obama '09	12,867	14,234	90%
	1,565	3,844	41%				2009 is projected
	1,817	4,149	44%			*In Billions of Dollars*	
	2,121	4,409	48%				
	2,346	4,655	50%		Figures do not include $35 - 50 trillion in		
	2,601	5,012	52%		Social Security and Medicare obligations		

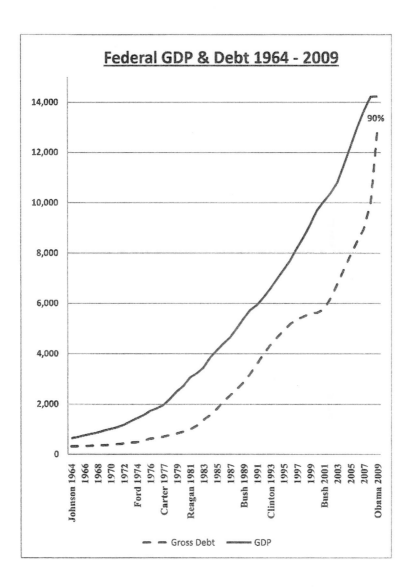

Federal GDP & Debt 1964 - 2009

Tea Partiers already see the consequences of fiscal irresponsibility. Future historians and economists will record that the collapse of the United States' economy, the devaluation of the American dollar, and the end of our superpower status was caused by the fiscal irresponsibility by members of the United States Congress, as well as U.S. presidents who refused to use their veto power—*not* al-Qaeda.

U.S. debt at the end of:

- Mr. Clinton's term = $5 trillion: We would have to pay $29,977,526,257 per month for 30 years to retire this debt, which is $360 billion per year, principal and interest.
- Mr. Bush's term = $10 trillion: We would have to pay $59,955,052,515 per month for 30 years to retire this debt, which is $719 billion per year, principal and interest.
- Mr. Obama's term = $14 trillion: We would have to pay $83,937,073,521 per month for 30 years to retire this debt, which is $1 trillion per year, principal and interest.

The U.S. government takes in $2.5 trillion per year, and the current debt payback will equal $1 trillion per year. Hence, the U.S. government *cannot* meet its fiscal obligations with current receipts and levels of spending. The important thing to remember is not that our past three presidents announced plans to eliminate the <u>deficit</u>, which is a daily or monthly figure. However, the real goal should be eliminating the <u>debt</u>, which is the total accumulation of all preceding deficits.

The average American citizen is fiscally conservative. We make money by working in a small business or corporation. We ensure that our rent, mortgage, utilities, and food do not exceed our income. Americans with high-school educations know how to balance their checkbooks. Why don't our elected officials?

> *The imposition of heavy taxes is a limit on man's freedom.*
> —Barry Goldwater (1964)

Graduated Taxes and Who Pays the Debt

Total debt and excess spending is not the only issue. Graduated taxes are inherently unfair due to unequal treatment of U.S. taxpayers.

Income	SE Tax	Fed Inc Tax	State TX	Total Tax	Tax Rate
$ 4,000	565	-	-	565	14%
$ 10,000	1,413	383	178	1,974	20%
$ 20,000	2,826	1,568	609	5,003	25%
$ 30,000	4,239	2,963	1,039	8,241	27%
$ 40,000	5,652	4,358	1,470	11,480	29%
$ 50,000	7,065	6,600	1,901	15,566	31%
$ 60,000	8,478	8,925	2,329	19,732	33%
$ 70,000	9,891	11,250	2,760	23,901	34%
$ 80,000	11,304	13,563	3,190	28,057	35%
$ 90,000	12,717	15,888	3,620	32,225	36%
$ 100,000	14,130	18,471	4,051	36,652	37%

This table shows income levels from $4,000 to $100,000, along with associated Self-Employment Tax (SE Tax), Federal Income Tax, and a representative State Income Tax using 2008 tax tables.

Fairness could be construed as all taxpayers paying

the exact same *amount* of taxes, which would be difficult for those with lower income levels. (E.g., If the government spends $3 trillion per year, and has 300 million citizens, then each citizen would owe $10,000 annually; a family of four would owe $40,000, etc.)

Alternatively, "fairness" could be defined as all wage earners paying exactly the same *rate*. However, fairness under the law cannot be defined as some taxpayers paying nothing, while others pay 14 percent, and still others carry a 37 percent tax burden. One taxpayer cannot get 23 percent more benefit than another, so payments should be at equal percentages.

If all citizens are supposed to be treated equally, why is the tax code written so that a citizen earning $4,000 pays 14 percent of wages in taxes, but a citizen who earns $100,000 pays a rate of 37 percent?

Remember the Karl Marx quote? *"From each according to his abilities, to each according to his needs."* When graduated taxes were enacted, the political elites' intent was social engineering that reduced high achievers to a lower level of income in the name of fairness. The actual result has been to discourage high achievement.

Tea Partiers know that we must eliminate social engineering in the tax code. Citizens are <u>not</u> guinea pigs. Adopt a 10 percent flat tax, which provides a sufficient amount of revenue for all constitutionally mandated functions of the federal government. We could then abolish all tax tables, along with the Internal Revenue Service (IRS).

Thousands of former IRS agents could then be retrained to independently audit all elected officials and all government programs on an annual basis to eliminate mismanagement, cheating, fraud, waste, and abuse.

Social Security – The Federal Government's Ponzi Scheme

Ponzi was a scammer who promised investors 100 percent returns on their investments within 90 days. He used the deposits from new investors to pay the returns on the earlier investors, essentially "robbing Peter to pay Paul." Eventually, his house of cards crashed when new investments could not keep pace with paying returns to early investors.

In a similar manner, the United States government created Social Security. Although originally promising to use a "pay as you go" system, the taxpayers' Social Security contributions were combined with the general revenue fund in 1968. The Johnson administration did this during the buildup of the Vietnam War, and our retirement funds have been spent on many different projects unrelated to retirement. Excess Social Security taxes are borrowed by the government to finance other spending.

Here is the rub: If you invested 15 percent of your paycheck over a 45-year period, you would be a millionaire! Instead, the federal government deducts Social Security taxes from our paychecks and provides those funds to today's retirees. The funds are not stored in an interest-bearing savings account and the Social Security lockbox is fictitious.

So what does this mean to us as taxpayers? It means a lot. Please look at the chart on the adjacent page. E.g., If you use the median income from 1964 to 2009, you would have earned $1,414,649 in lifetime earnings. You contribute 6.2 percent to Social Security and 1.5 percent to Medicare; in addition, your employer contributes a matching amount. So the total for both insurance plans is just over 15 percent. If you are taxed at 15 percent of income for 45 years, your forfeited wages would be $212,197, which is represented by the small peak on the lower line in 2009. The trend line drops rapidly, assuming that you begin to draw Social Security checks for $20,000 per year.

In contrast, if every worker in America were able to self-invest 15 percent per year in a mutual fund, then they would each have $1,126,971 in investments ($212,197 principal and $914,774 interest), with the historical interest rate of 8 percent. At this rate, every retiree would be able to draw out $120,000 per year, as represented by the top line on the graph.

The real question each of us must ask is whether we, as wage earners and taxpayers, would rather have the Social Security "ponzi" check for $20,000 per year or the mutual fund check for $120,000 per year. Tea Partiers know that Social Security is *not* a good deal. The government not only confiscates 15 percent of our income, but we also lose the potential dividends and interest that could make every American a millionaire!

In addition, the question of whether Social Security is constitutional has never been resolved. Yes, the Supreme Court made a decision that Social Security's taxes were valid exercises of the taxing power in Article I, Section 8, but the Court ducked the primary issue of whether Social Security is an *unconstitutional* government insurance program. History books reveal that the Supreme Court was bullied and intimidated by Franklin D. Roosevelt ... and cowardice or political expediency reigned.

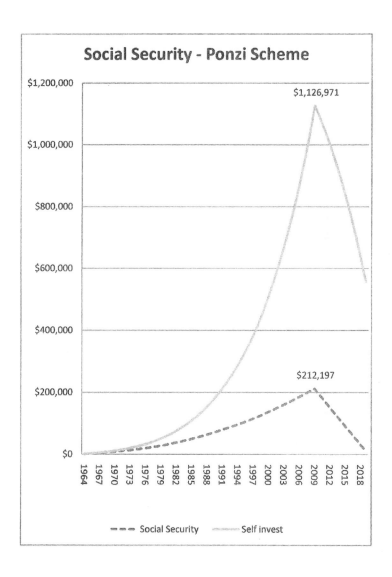

Social Security - Ponzi Scheme

This constitutional issue needs to be addressed again in light of 78 million baby boomers who will retire in the next 20 years, and the total liabilities and unfunded promises for Social Security and Medicare of $53 trillion. Tea Partiers know that the Framers did not intend for the federal government to bankrupt our country.

> *A wise and frugal government, which shall leave men free to regulate their own pursuits of industry and improvement, and shall not take from the mouth of labor the bread it has earned - this is the sum of good government.* .   —Thomas Jefferson

CHAPTER 6

The Welfare State

The president is not Robin Hood! The U.S. Constitution does not authorize redistribution of wealth.

There are several Robin Hood fables, and in a common version of the tale, the Sheriff of Nottingham and tax collectors steal from the common people on behalf of the crooked King John, and Robin Hood returns the money to the people. Robin is not viewed as a hoodlum by citizens of Sherwood Forest, because he is merely returning to them what was illegally confiscated.

The federal government under several administrations, but most recently under Bush and Obama, have been taking money from the people and redistributing it to individuals, multimillion dollar corporations, banks, and foreign governments. The key point is that neither Bush nor Obama are Robin Hood—they are both modern-day versions of the greedy King John.

Socialistic-Progressives have created "serfs" by institutionalizing a drug-like addiction to allegedly "free" federal benefits that are unearned. Simultaneously, they create victims of the working class and small businesses through unusually high tax burdens. The demise of the Soviet Empire was primarily due to economic collapse. The leaders of the Former Soviet Union (FSU) came to realize that a command-directed economy did not work. Despite that history lesson, American Socialistic-Progressives continue to push the United States into socialism through the welfare state.

Individual Welfare

High taxes and complicated regulations cause slower business growth and, therefore, result in higher unemployment. Similarly, higher taxes increase the cost of doing business and reduce the number of employees that could otherwise be hired. If the government concentrated on reducing regulations while prosecuting white-collar criminals for fraud, then employment would increase.

Tea Partiers know politicians are lying when they say the government has created a number of jobs. The government does not create jobs! It can merely improve the legal and regulatory environment in which private investors create businesses and jobs.

Welfare Example				
SSI	1361/mo	$	1,361	
WIC	400/child	$	1,600	
Food Stamps	250/wk	$	1,000	
		$	3,961	per month
			x 12	mos
		$	47,532	per year
			x 1 million	recipients
		$	47,532,000,000	Annually

Welfare is loosely defined as unearned entitlements or charity. Charity is not listed in the U.S. Constitution, and should, therefore, be a function left to the decision of the various states, people, or private charities.

Tea Partiers understand that these benefits are intended for citizens who are temporarily out of work. In the hypothetical example, if a million people received these benefits, this would cost over $47 billion per year. But Tea Partiers want to know why our taxes are transferred to support noncitizens and illegal immigrants. This practice needs to end now!

Corporate Welfare

The Founding Fathers did *not* support corporate welfare. Yet, today, billions are being spent on "corporate welfare" whereby the government is taking from the taxpayer and redistributing wealth to corporations. This practice needs to end.

The most recent form of insanity and arrogance involved the Bush and Obama bailouts of mortgage lending institutions and insurance companies. Individual taxpayers did not receive a dividend check from these corporations when they made billions in profit. Hence, taxpayers should not be *forced* to bail out failed businesses by political edict. Tea Partiers recognize this bailout as legalized theft of the U.S. Treasury.

Since corporate welfare is not enumerated in the Constitution, it should be eliminated immediately. Bailouts will be discussed more in Chapter 7.

Foreign Aid Is Welfare

In addition to welfare for individuals and corporations, the federal government created something called foreign aid. Foreign aid is "welfare" for other countries, whereby the president and secretary of state take money from the American taxpayer and provide monetary and other gifts to foreign nations. The reality is that much of this money is never seen by citizens of other nations, and it often becomes "free money" for the whims of their political elites.

During his Inaugural Address, Mr. Obama stated this support of taking from American taxpayers to provide foreign welfare:

> *"To the people of poor nations, we pledge to work alongside you to make your farms flourish and let clean waters flow; to nourish starved bodies and feed hungry minds."* —Barack Obama, Jan 20, 2009

Similarly, during a recent speech in Ghana, he said "My administration has committed $63 billion to meet [Africa's health] challenges—$63 billion! Building on the strong efforts of President Bush, we will carry forward the fight against HIV/AIDS."

This is a commendable humanitarian goal, but this is not authorized in the United States Constitution. In fact, foreign aid increased substantially during the Bush administration as well, and it, too, was an unlawful confiscation and redistribution of taxpayer wealth. Playing Robin Hood with taxpayer dollars for foreign beneficiaries should be an impeachable offense.

So should aiding and abetting a terrorist organization.

In March 2009, Secretary of State Hillary Clinton pledged $300 million of our tax dollars to rebuild HAMAS-controlled Gaza. Yet, HAMAS (Islamic Resistance Movement) is a terrorist organization consistently listed in the Department of State's "Patterns of Global Terrorism" and their "List of Designated Foreign Terrorist Organizations." Why are American taxpayers being forced to fund terrorists?

Socialistic-Progressives want greater state control of the economy so that they (not you and I) can dictate who gets what, and how much. Every dollar that goes to individual welfare, corporate welfare, and foreign aid is taken from the U.S. taxpayer, subordinating our citizens to these special interests.

Do we officially become serfs or indentured servants when our tax rate hits 40 percent or 50 percent?

At a tax rate of 51 percent, should we change our designation from citizen to comrade? Washington, Adams, Jefferson, and Franklin were opposed to confiscatory taxes, deficit spending, and redistribution of wealth. They also spoke against saddling future generations with our debts. Yet, for the past forty-five years, our presidents and our Congress have continued the unconstitutional move toward socialism and the welfare state. Here is the rub: socialistic-progressives want a benevolent dictator with monarch-like powers; but, Tea Partiers want a return to our Constitutional Republic.

"... as all history informs us, there has been in every State & Kingdom a constant kind of warfare between the governing & governed: the one striving to obtain more for its support, and the other to pay less. And this has alone occasioned great convulsions, actual civil wars, ending either in dethroning of the Princes, or enslaving of the people. Generally indeed the ruling power carries its point, the revenues of princes constantly increasing, and we see that they are never satisfied, but always in want of more. The more the people are discontented with the oppression of taxes; the greater need the prince has of money to distribute among his partisans and pay the troops that are to suppress all resistance, and enable him to plunder at pleasure. There is scarce a king in a hundred who would not, if he could, follow the example of Pharaoh, get first all the people's money, then all their lands, and then make them and their children servants for ever ..."

—Benjamin Franklin (June 2, 1787)

CHAPTER 7

Eschew Obfuscation

"Eschew obfuscation" in plain English means that the government should avoid ambiguity and adopt clarity. For greatest clarity or transparency, every law should have a tie to the powers granted to the federal government within the U.S. Constitution. Politicians rely upon confusion and obfuscation—the more complicated they make a concept sound, the harder it is for taxpayers to challenge.

During the Bush and Obama administrations, the federal government has consistently obfuscated the facts. During Bush's campaign, he adopted the typical mantras of conservatism: reduced spending, balanced budget, smaller government, and greater freedom. Mr. Bush's results are the opposite and his enduring legacy is a larger federal government and a monstrously large debt; unfortunately, Obama's fiscal policies did not pull us away from Bush's fiscal precipice; instead they pushed taxpayers and future generations into the abyss.

Reduced Spending and Balanced Budget

During the Viet Nam conflict, an unnamed major allegedly spoke about the battle at Ben Tre, saying, "It became necessary to destroy the town in order to save it." The claim that the destruction of a town served a greater good for the citizens of that town and all concerned was not the perspective of the residents, home owners, and shop owners of Ben Tre, Viet Nam. In a similar sense of faulty logic, Mr. Bush announced to CNN that "I've abandoned free-market principles to save the free-market system." This is as absurd as the military quote and reveals the true George W. Bush: a Big-Government politician who believed that more federal spending will solve all problems. Eschew obfuscation!

> *"I've abandoned free-market principles to save the free-market system"* —George W. Bush (Dec. 2008)

Similarly and without apology, Mr. Bush created a prescription benefit program that substantially increased federal spending in the health-care arena, clearly an unconstitutional federal role. Buying votes through pork barrel spending during the Bush administration exceeded any fiscal conservative's tolerance level. As described in Chapter 5, Mr. Bush started with a federal debt of just over $5 trillion and completed his eight-year tenure with a debt of over $10 trillion, which was almost a 100 percent increase, yet only a fraction of this amount is directly attributed to the War on Terror.

By any *fiscal* measure, Mr. Bush was the first Socialist president of the United States in the 21st century. Furthermore, he and his administration never addressed the rising Medicare, Medicaid, and Social Security debt, which are estimated between $35 to $50 trillion dollars, depending upon which reference one uses.

In addition, Mr. Obama has repeatedly said that he inherited a massive deficit from the Bush administration. This is disingenuous, because as a senator, he helped vote it into law.

Eschew obfuscation: Tea Partiers view deficit spending as a stealth tax—a coward's way of increasing taxes on the next generation.

Smaller Government and Greater Freedom

Mr. Bush's reaction to the 9/11 attacks was to increase the size and role of the federal government. Systemically, the success of the 9/11 terrorist attacks was a failure to share information between federal departments and agencies with their counterparts at the state and local levels. Yet, creation of the Department of Homeland Security (DHS) and the Transportation Security Agency (TSA) substantially increased the number and cost of federal employees without fully addressing that root cause. In addition, Bush signed the Uniting and Strengthening America by Providing Appropriate Tools Required to Intercept and Obstruct Terrorism Act (USA PATRIOT Act) into law 43 days after the terrorist attacks.

The PATRIOT Act allegedly streamlined communications between agencies; but it also violated important tenets guaranteed by our Bill of Rights, which were designed to prevent abuse of power. "Sneak-and-peek" searches were considered one of the most egregious provisions, unconstitutionally undermining the protection of the Fourth

Amendment of the Constitution.

Eschew obfuscation: Tea Partiers know that freedom is not improved by a reduction in individual rights.

> *Any society that would give up a little liberty to gain a little security will deserve neither and lose both.*
> —Benjamin Franklin

Troubled Asset Relief Program (TARP)

The Troubled Asset Relief Program (TARP) is a program of the United States government to purchase assets and equity from financial institutions to strengthen its financial sector. It is the largest component of the government's measures in 2008 to address the subprime mortgage crisis. Eschew obfuscation! The federal government is taking taxpayer money to bail out millionaires who made bad corporate investments.

- # 1: Amendments to the Community Reinvestment Act (CRA) during the 1990s resulted in relaxed mortgage lending standards.
- # 2: Fannie Mae and Freddie Mac, both quasi-government agencies, began making subprime (risky) loans to borrowers with poor credit. (They are often referred to as government-sponsored enterprises.)
- # 3: The Clinton administration threatened litigation if banks did not have equity in outcome; this caused banks to adopt risky loan standards.

- # 4: People got greedy. A low-income or very low-income borrower who may have qualified for a $100,000 mortgage loan was being approved for loans that were two or three times higher than salaries justified in the name of social equality.
- # 5: The Bush administration did not correct the loan standards. Housing sales increased during the boom; then the economy and housing market contracted, and many of the low-income borrowers merely walked away, placing their loans in default.
- # 6: Many financial institutions had "bundled" risky mortgage loans with creditworthy loans; hence, the entire financial bundle was at risk.
- # 7: To mitigate risk, the financial community created something called a credit-default swap (CDS), which was a type of insurance plan. (E.g., Bear Sterns paid AIG a premium, and AIG guaranteed payment if the loan defaults).
- # 8: When the economy contracted, the housing bubble burst and the risky loans began defaulting.
- # 9: Fannie Mae, Freddie Mac, and numerous other financial institutions were left holding "bad loans" due to poor credit risks and asked AIG to provide CDS insurance payments. AIG couldn't.
- # 10: The federal government created the risky-loan initiatives in the 1990s; then they intervened in 2008 and 2009 to bail out the millionaires who made poor decisions, wasting billions of taxpayer money.
- #11: The Federal Reserve funded AIG and Bear Stearns, allowing Lehman Brothers to fail, which means the Fed is picking the winners and losers

rather than the free market.

- #12: The Bush administration provided $700 billion to the treasury secretary that was used to nationalize many large banks.
- #13: The Obama administration made matters worse by pushing through an $800 billion spending bill without any accountability to the American people.
- #14: Bush and Obama nationalized General Motors and Chrysler Corporation by converting government loans into equity—hence, as the "owner" of these large corporations, the federal government has assumed responsibility for their health-care contracts, a potential hidden agenda.

The middle class did not receive multi-million dollar bonuses common to financial executives during the boom years; but as a result of federal government bailouts, taxpayers have been saddled with billions in toxic loans that might never be repaid. The Big Government Socialists and Progressives in the Bush and Obama administrations decided that free market economics don't work, taking money from hard-working Americans and giving it to failed leaders of unprofitable companies. Our key message to the deadbeat borrowers, bankers, and politicians: Just because you screwed up does not make your bad debts the taxpayers' responsibility!

Eschew obfuscation: Financial Industry Regulatory Authority (ww.FINRA.org) is an independent regulatory organization empowered by the federal government to ensure that America's 90 million investors are protected. FINRA didn't. So why should we trust even more money to

Big Government? Legalized theft is not a federal power enumerated in the U.S. Constitution.

Cap and Trade (a.k.a. Cap and Tax)

Cap and trade is a program that is supposed to help limit carbon emissions; the net effect of cap and trade will be a substantial increase in taxes for all Americans.

Cap refers to a maximum amount of pollution that a company could produce. The "cap" amount will be determined by a politician or political body, and not all caps will be equal. For instance, will a cap be the same for a utility company that uses coal versus one that uses hydro or nuclear power?

Trade refers to an exchange or sale of credits. For instance, assume that three utility companies are all authorized a cap of 100 credits. If pollution from Company "A" scores 100, Company "B" scores 125 points, and Company "C" scores 75 points, then A is neutral, B must buy 25 points, and C can sell or trade 25 points.

The Cap and Trade Tax would not be an outright transfer of money from B to C, but would result in the redistribution of wealth for other government programs. The federal government would be the broker, skimming a portion of this tax to feed federal bureaucracy.

Communities with older technology in their power plants will end up continuously buying credits, thereby reducing the amount of retained earnings they would potentially reinvest. Communities that rely upon fossil fuels would be hardest hit—electricity rates will skyrocket. Rural communities will be hit harder than big cities, because "per capita" calculations would increase costs on Wyoming taxpayers greater than residents of large-population states such as New York or California. What do we get in return? Not much. Sovereignty concerns arise from potential measuring, reporting, verification, and enforcement by international bodies. Are we expected to surrender to international organizations? How much of this new tax will be transferred from American wage earners to international bodies? In addition, if countries like China do not have cap and trade taxes, then their cost of manufacturing is cheaper than American costs. This places all American manufacturers in a weaker position than the big polluters in China.

Eschew obfuscation: Tea Partiers know that this is a significant utility tax increase with estimates of $100–200 billion per year. Politicians aren't honest enough to tell us that they want to enact substantially higher taxes on utility companies, which will be passed on to consumers. Instead, they express concern over the environment while trying to obfuscate costs to American taxpayers.

Health Care

The President and Congress need to ask *the* right question: *Not how, but should?*

The real question isn't "how" to provide equal health care to everyone, but "should" citizens authorize the federal government to expand its power through a new amendment to the U.S. Constitution that authorizes governance over health care.

Every citizen has the right to purchase their own health care; but socialized health care is not a federal power enumerated in the U.S. Constitution. Medicare and

Medicaid health insurance programs were never authorized through a constitutional amendment. But, Mr. Obama is not seeking an amendment to legitimize his vision of socialized, government-controlled medicine.

Before the first question can be answered by an informed public, we need to look at the history of health care spending by the federal government. It is unfortunate for the American taxpayer that the federal government's involvement in health care already consumes billions of dollars of our money. Here are a few facts:

- In 1964, the federal government spent $4.6 billion per year on Health and Human Services (to include Medicare and Medicaid), which came to $24 per capita in spending
- Based on inflation rates, the $4.6 billion equates to $31.9 billion in 2009
- Today, the federal government spends $780 billion per year on Health and Human Services (to include Medicare and Medicaid), which comes to $2,570 per capita in spending

Tea Partiers can do the math, so why can't our politicians? Between 1964 and 2009, our population increased from 191.9 million to 303.8 million, representing an increase of 58 percent. During the same time period, federal spending on Health and Human Services rose from $4.6 billion to over $780 billion, representing an increase of 10,597 percent. Although the rate of inflation changed by 595 percent, our federal spending was an insane 10,000 percent increase. This is proof-positive that the federal government is incapable of controlling costs related to health care.

Emotionally based arguments for more money do not erase the fact that the federal government has <u>not</u> earned the trust of the already overburdened taxpayer. Mr. Obama stated that two-thirds of the cost of his new health-care plan could be recouped from Medicare and Medicaid. A more prudent course of action would be to improve efficiency, costs, and coverage in Medicare and Medicaid, while simultaneously seeking an amendment to the Constitution authorizing federal government intrusion. This course of action would simultaneously earn the trust and respect of the American people and fulfill Mr. Obama's oath to preserve and protect the Constitution. However, Mr. Obama stated:

> "The plan I'm announcing would meet three basic goals. It will provide more security and stability to those who have health insurance. It will provide insurance for those who don't. It will slow the growth of health-care costs for our families, our businesses, and our government." (09/09/09)

He lied: Mr. Obama stated that his plan would be revenue neutral—not adding a cent to the deficit, which is not fiscally possible. The government cannot increase spending for the health care of 30 million people without increasing cost. This is an intellectually dishonest promise of hope over reality. Anyone with an ounce of common sense can spot a snake oil sales pitch; unfortunately, few of our elected officials possess one ounce.

On September 9, 2009, during a televised speech, Mr. Obama stated, "The plan will not add to our deficit. The middle class will realize greater security, not higher taxes.

And if we are able to slow the growth of health-care costs by just one-tenth of 1 percent each year, it will actually reduce the deficit by $4 trillion over the long term."

Let's do the math:

$2,000,000,000,000 X 0.10% = $2,000,000,000

(two trillion X 0.10% = two billion)

If we save one-tenth of 1 percent each year, it would take 2,000 years to reduce the deficit by $4 trillion. Do they teach math at Occidental College, Columbia University, or Harvard Law School? Tea Partiers want to know why you and your staff can't do 8th grade math?

Mr. Obama outlined that he would save between 300 to 500 billion dollars from the current Medicare and Medicaid budgets. But, the Congressional Budget Office Director Douglas W. Elmendorf stated that "little reliable evidence exists about exactly how to implement those types of changes." In addition, the CBO projections for these budgets are grim:

	2009	2019
Medicare	$422.0 billion	$797.1 billion
Medicaid	$255.4 billion	$426.1 billion
	$677.4 billion	$1223.2 billion

This is an 81% increase in just 10 years! If the Big Government politicians cannot control costs for these existing programs, why should taxpayers surrender more money and more authority to these people? Although Mr. Obama said illegal immigrants would not be covered by his plan, he did not explain his plans for making law-breakers American citizens. In addition, Mr. Obama needs to address tort reform, medical malpractice damage awards, as well as whistleblower protection.

Eschew obfuscation: Tea Partiers know that expansion of the federal government into the health-care sector and adding 30 million new beneficiaries will <u>not</u> help lower costs or improve benefits for our citizens.

> *It only stands to reason that where there's sacrifice, there's someone collecting the sacrificial offerings. Where there's service, there is someone being served. The man who speaks to you of sacrifice is speaking of slaves and masters, and intends to be the master.*
>
> —Ayn Rand

Whistleblower Protection Act

During Mr. Obama's televised health-care speech, he also stated:

First, I will not sign a plan that adds one dime to our deficits—either now or in the future. Period …

Second, we've estimated that most of this plan can be paid for by finding savings within the existing health-care system—a system that is currently full of *waste and abuse*.

The Federal Whistleblower Protection Act does not protect whistleblowers effectively. When a whistleblower brings forth evidence, many face unethical and frivolous lawsuits by large corporations that make false accusations of slander, defamation, or loss of privacy. The whistleblower is often fired and driven into bankruptcy due to court costs to prove their honesty. At times, large corporations will intimidate a whistleblower through a lawsuit; and when the whistleblower is about to face financial collapse due to mounting legal defense costs against baseless allegations, the corporation will offer an out-of-court settlement to silence the truth.

Eschew obfuscation: Tea Partiers know that waste and abuse will not be eliminated until whistleblowers are protected from the wrongdoers. No whistleblower should face bankruptcy for doing what is legally and ethically correct.

> *The only thing necessary for the triumph of evil is for good men to do nothing.*
> —Edmund Burke

Robbing Peter to Pay for Paul's Car

The federal government dreamed up yet another scheme that cannot be supported by either the Constitution or common sense. The Car Allowance Rebate System (CARS) is commonly known as the "Cash for Clunkers" program. Buyers could obtain a $3,500 or $4,500 credit, depending on the type of vehicles traded in, the type of vehicles purchased, with guidance on fuel economy. Three billion dollars funded rebates on almost 700,000 cars. One goal of this Socialist bill was to help Detroit's manufacturers, yet over 40 percent of the sales revenues went to Japanese manufacturers. Why wasn't a "Buy American" clause added to this dubious bill since the federal government took taxpayer money from Persons A through Y to pay for Person Z's car?

Eschew obfuscation: Transferring money from Person A's earnings to Person B's car payments is yet another indicator that the federal government has been seized by

Socialists. Our Founding Fathers would be enraged at this theft and transfer of taxpayer's dollars.

> *Political freedom means the absence of coercion*
> *of a man by his fellow men.*
> —Milton Friedman (1962)

Read the Bills!

Whether it is the USA PATRIOT Act or the Obama Health Care Act, every elected official should be required to read every paragraph of every bill. If they don't, then how does an elected official know what he/she is voting upon?

In July 2009, House Majority Leader Mr. Steny Hoyer stated that "If every member pledged to not vote for it if they hadn't read it in its entirety, I think we would have very few votes."

Similarly, Mr. John Conyers, a Michigan congressman and the chairman of the House Judiciary Committee, protested against the concept of reading each bill: "To get up and say, 'Read the bill.' What good is reading the bill if it's 1,000 pages and you don't have two days and two lawyers to find out what it means after you read the bill?"

These two quotes reveal how very broken the federal government has become.

Eschew obfuscation: Reading each bill must be mandatory! In addition, every bill should focus on one topic at a time so that pork is not bundled with good legislation.

CHAPTER **8**

The Way Ahead

Tea Partiers are finally trying to accomplish the same goals and objectives that Barry Goldwater envisioned 45 years ago:

- Adherence to the Constitution
- Shrink the size of the federal government
- Return to state's rights and authority
- Protection of individual rights and freedoms
- Fiscal responsibility

Tea Partiers' goal in the *short term* must notify the current president and U.S. Congress that socialized health care is not a constitutionally authorized function without an amendment. They have a choice to initiate the amendment process or face defeat in the next election.

Next, we must bring new people into the U.S. Congress to fix the mess that has been made by our elected officials since 1964. Once all incumbents with socialist beliefs have been replaced, then we need to hold the newly elected officials accountable and create an amendment limiting number of terms.

Tea Partiers believe that our politicians should individually and collectively show responsibility and integrity. There is a nexus between religious principles and United States Code in that both condemn lies, thefts or stealing, and murder. There are state and local ordinances against adultery as well.

In cases where our elected officials lie to us or steal from us, they should be prosecuted. In cases where the president or members of Congress commit a felony, they should face impeachment, a trial, and the same prison sentence as any other citizen. No elected official should ever receive a "Get Out of Jail Free" card. This isn't Monopoly. Without regard for race, creed, color or party affiliation:

- If the President commits perjury, prosecute him!
- If the Congressman cheats on his taxes, prosecute him!
- If the Secretary of the Treasury or the Chairman of the Ways & Means Committee cheats on their taxes, fire them!
- If elected officials violate our Bill of Rights, get rid of them!
- If our officials violate the oath to protect and defend the Constitution, get rid of them!

Finally, to ensure the financial survival of our nation, we must repeal the federal income tax, dismantle all unconstitutional organizations and programs, adopt a balanced budget amendment, and eliminate all forms of welfare at the federal level within the next two to four years.

The road to a balanced budget, smaller government, and a constitutionally guided Republic will be a tough one. Our government and both major parties have been infiltrated by Socialists and Progressives, who do not want to give up the power to tax, spend, control, and dictate mandates from Washington, D.C. Survival of our nation and prosperity for our children dictates our stand against all enemies, foreign or domestic. In 1690, John Locke wrote, "The reason why men enter into society, is the preservation of their property; (But) whenever the legislators endeavour to take away, and destroy the property of the people, or to reduce them to slavery under arbitrary power, they put themselves into a state of war with the people." The Speaker of the House and other politicians who are opposed to constitutional compliance are by definition domestic enemies who must be defeated by patriotic voters.

> *The tree of liberty must be refreshed from time to time with the blood of patriots and tyrants.*
> —Thomas Jefferson

Tea Party Revival has focused upon constitutional amendments, fiscal responsibility, and facts that outline the incompetence and excesses of the federal government. We are focused upon fiscal facts, not political fantasies. And "hope" is not a strategy.

Some Tea Partiers are religious, and others are not. We close with a biblical quote related to deficit spending and debt. This verse was written by Solomon, the son of David, and is dedicated to the Big Government bailout advocates of the Bush and Obama administrations:

Proverbs—"<u>Don't Be Foolish</u>" (Contemporary English Version)

6.1. My child, suppose you agree to pay the debt of someone who cannot repay a loan.

6.2. Then you are trapped by your own words,

6.3. And you are now in the power of someone else. Here is what you should do: Go and beg for permission to call off the agreement.

6.4. Do this before you fall asleep or even get sleepy.

6.5. Save yourself, just as a deer or a bird tries to escape from a hunter.

17.18. It's stupid to guarantee someone else's loan.

One may disagree with portions of this book,
but Solomon's wisdom remains sound.

AFTERWORD

During the editing of Tea Party Revival, Jimmy Carter, was asked about opposition to the President's policies. He stated on national television, "I think an overwhelming portion of the intensely demonstrated animosity toward President Barack Obama is based on the fact that he is a black man … because of the belief among many white people … that African Americans are not qualified to lead this great country."

This type of destructive comment is not based on fact, but based upon Carter's own bias, his lack of knowledge, or his lack of morality. Exaggerated or false allegations of racism by this former president have eliminated the last shreds of his credibility. Carter, who portrays himself as a born-again Christian, would do well to reread his Bible and review Proverbs 4:24 "Never tell lies or be deceitful in what you say."

Like many politicians, Carter doesn't get it. The only color that Tea Partiers are concerned with is the monstrously large RED figures on the federal government's balance sheets: we prefer black and white. Tea Partiers have been consistent in our opposition to unconstitutional growth of Big Government, higher taxes, deficit spending and fiscally irresponsible debts. Disagreement with socialistic fiscal policy is not racist! We don't care what color a cat is, as long as it catches mice!

Finally, the current fiscal mess was NOT caused by capitalism. As described herein, it was caused by Big Government politicians who lacked honesty and transparency; meddled in the housing market; failed to monitor and regulate Credit Default Swaps; failed to balance the federal budget; taxed many citizens to pay off a few millionaires; strayed from constitutional compliance; and boiled our American frogs. If we get government out of manipulating and over-taxing the economy, then Adam Smith's invisible hand of economics will restore this nation to prosperity. Capitalism is not the cause of the crisis, it is the cure.

> *Political freedom is tied to economic freedom. As a parent, I am outraged that our Big Government politicians have created indentured servants out of taxpayers, our children, and grandchildren through reckless, unconstrained spending. It is time to take our country back.*
>
> —Dr. B. Leland Baker

FURTHER RESEARCH

If you believe in smaller government and greater liberty, then you may wish to investigate one or more of these Web sites:

The Libertarian Party	www.lp.org
The CATO Institute	www.cato.org
Big Government	biggovernment.com/
Campaign For Liberty	www.campaignforliberty.com
Citizens Against Government Waste	www.cagw.org
Freedom Works	www.freedomworks.org
National Taxpayer Union	www.ntu.org
Reason Magazine	www.reason.com
The Ayn Rand Institute	www.aynrand.org
The Constitution Party	www.constitutionparty.com
The Heritage Foundation	www.heritage.org
The John Birch Society	www.jbs.org
The Objective Standard	www.theobjectivestandard.com
Downsizer Dispatch	downsizer-dispatch@downsizedc.org

912 Organizers	
American Conservative Union	www.conservative.org/
American Liberty Alliance	americanlibertyalliance.com/
Americans for Tax Reform	www.atr.org/
Ayn Rand Center	www.aynrand.org
Bureau Crash	bureaucrash.com/
Campaign for Liberty	www.campaignforliberty.com/
Center for Individual Freedom	cfif.org/
Citizens Against Government Waste	www.cagw.org/site/PageServer
Competitive Enterprise Institute	cei.org/about
Free Republic	www.freerepublic.com/
Freedom Works Foundation	www.freedomworks.org/
Grassfire	www.grassfire.org/index.htm
Heartland Institute	www.heartland.org/
Institute For Liberty	www.instituteforliberty.org/
Jews for Preservation of Firearms	www.jpfo.org
Let Freedom Ring	www.letfreedomringusa.com/
National Taxpayers Union	www.ntu.org/main/
ParcBench	www.parcbench.com/
Patrick Henry Center	www.patrickhenrycenter.com/
ResistNet	www.resistnet.com/
Right March	www.rightmarch.com/
Smart Girl Politics	www.smartgirlpolitics.org/
Tea Party Nation	www.teapartynation.com/
Tea Party Patriots	www.teapartypatriots.org/
The Club for Growth	www.clubforgrowth.org/
The Leadership Institute	www.leadershipinstitute.org/
We the People Revolution	www.wethepeoplerevolution.com
Young America's Foundation	www.yaf.org/
Young Americans for Liberty	www.yaliberty.org/
Our Country Deserves Better	www.ourcountrydeservesbetter.com

The United States Constitution

The United States Constitution

We the People of the United States, in Order to form a more perfect Union, establish Justice, insure domestic Tranquility, provide for the common defence, promote the general Welfare, and secure the Blessings of Liberty to ourselves and our Posterity, do ordain and establish this Constitution for the United States of America.

Article I

SECTION 1

All legislative Powers herein granted shall be vested in a Congress of the United States, which shall consist of a Senate and House of Representatives.

SECTION 2

The House of Representatives shall be composed of Members chosen every second Year by the People of the several States, and the Electors in each State shall have the Qualifications requisite for Electors of the most numerous Branch of the State Legislature.

No Person shall be a Representative who shall not have attained to the Age of twenty five Years, and been seven Years a Citizen of the United States, and who shall not, when elected, be an Inhabitant of that State in which he shall be chosen.

Representatives and direct Taxes shall be apportioned

among the several States which may be included within this Union, according to their respective Numbers, which shall be determined by adding to the whole Number of free Persons, including those bound to Service for a Term of Years, and excluding Indians not taxed, three fifths of all other Persons. The actual Enumeration shall be made within three Years after the first Meeting of the Congress of the United States, and within every subsequent Term of ten Years, in such Manner as they shall by Law direct. The Number of Representatives shall not exceed one for every thirty Thousand, but each State shall have at Least one Representative; and until such enumeration shall be made, the State of New Hampshire shall be entitled to chuse three, Massachusetts eight, Rhode-Island and Providence Plantations one, Connecticut five, New-York six, New Jersey four, Pennsylvania eight, Delaware one, Maryland six, Virginia ten, North Carolina five, South Carolina five, and Georgia three.

When vacancies happen in the Representation from any State, the Executive Authority thereof shall issue Writs of Election to fill such Vacancies.

The House of Representatives shall chuse their Speaker and other Officers; and shall have the sole Power of Impeachment.

SECTION 3

The Senate of the United States shall be composed of two Senators from each State, chosen by the Legislature thereof, for six Years; and each Senator shall have one Vote.

Immediately after they shall be assembled in Consequence of the first Election, they shall be divided as equally as may be into three Classes. The Seats of the Senators of the first Class shall be vacated at the Expiration of the second Year, of the second Class at the Expiration of the fourth Year, and of the third Class at the Expiration of the sixth Year, so that one third may be chosen every second Year; and if Vacancies happen by Resignation, or otherwise, during the Recess of the Legislature of any State, the Executive thereof may make temporary Appointments until the next Meeting of the Legislature, which shall then fill such Vacancies.

No Person shall be a Senator who shall not have attained to the Age of thirty Years, and been nine Years a Citizen of the United States, and who shall not, when elected, be an Inhabitant of that State for which he shall be chosen.

The Vice President of the United States shall be President of the Senate, but shall have no Vote, unless they be equally divided.

The Senate shall chuse their other Officers, and also a President pro tempore, in the Absence of the Vice President, or when he shall exercise the Office of President of the United States.

The Senate shall have the sole Power to try all Impeachments. When sitting for that Purpose, they shall be on Oath or Affirmation. When the President of the United States is tried, the Chief Justice shall preside: And no Person shall be convicted without the Concurrence of two thirds of the Members present.

Judgment in Cases of impeachment shall not extend further than to removal from Office, and disqualification to hold and enjoy any Office of honor, Trust or Profit under the United States: but the Party convicted shall nevertheless be liable and subject to Indictment, Trial, Judgment and Punishment, according to Law.

SECTION 4

The Times, Places and Manner of holding Elections for Senators and Representatives, shall be prescribed in each State by the Legislature thereof; but the Congress may at any time by Law make or alter such Regulations, except as to the Places of chusing Senators.

The Congress shall assemble at least once in every Year, and such Meeting shall be on the first Monday in December, unless they shall by Law appoint a different Day.

SECTION 5

Each House shall be the Judge of the Elections, Returns and Qualifications of its own Members, and a Majority of each shall constitute a Quorum to do Business; but a smaller Number may adjourn from day to day, and may be authorized to compel the Attendance of absent Members, in such Manner, and under such Penalties as each House may provide.

Each House may determine the Rules of its Proceedings, punish its Members for disorderly Behaviour, and, with the Concurrence of two thirds, expel a Member.

Each House shall keep a Journal of its Proceedings, and from time to time publish the same, excepting such Parts as may in their Judgment require Secrecy; and the Yeas and Nays of the Members of either House on any question shall, at the Desire of one fifth of those Present, be entered on the Journal.

Neither House, during the Session of Congress, shall,

without the Consent of the other, adjourn for more than three days, nor to any other Place than that in which the two Houses shall be sitting.

SECTION 6

The Senators and Representatives shall receive a Compensation for their Services, to be ascertained by Law, and paid out of the Treasury of the United States.6 They shall in all Cases, except Treason, Felony and Breach of the Peace, be privileged from Arrest during their Attendance at the Session of their respective Houses, and in going to and returning from the same; and for any Speech or Debate in either House, they shall not be questioned in any other Place.

No Senator or Representative shall, during the Time for which he was elected, be appointed to any civil Office under the Authority of the United States, which shall have been created, or the Emoluments whereof shall have been encreased during such time; and no Person holding any Office under the United States, shall be a Member of either House during his Continuance in Office.

SECTION 7

All Bills for raising Revenue shall originate in the House of Representatives; but the Senate may propose or concur with Amendments as on other Bills.

Every Bill which shall have passed the House of Representatives and the Senate, shall, before it become a Law, be presented to the President of the United States; If he approve he shall sign it, but if not he shall return it, with his Objections to that House in which it shall have originated, who shall enter the Objections at large on their Journal, and proceed to reconsider it. If after such Reconsideration two thirds of that House shall agree to pass the Bill, it shall be sent, together with the Objections, to the other House, by which it shall likewise be reconsidered, and if approved by two thirds of that House, it shall become a Law. But in all such Cases the Votes of both Houses shall be determined by yeas and Nays, and the Names of the Persons voting for and against the Bill shall be entered on the Journal of each House respectively. If any Bill shall not be returned by the President within ten Days (Sundays excepted) after it shall have been presented to him, the Same shall be a Law, in like Manner as if he had signed it, unless the Congress by their Adjournment prevent its Return, in which Case it shall not be a Law.

Every Order, Resolution, or Vote to which the Concurrence of the Senate and House of Representatives may be necessary (except on a question of Adjournment) shall be presented to the President of the United States; and before the Same shall take Effect, shall be approved by him, or being disapproved by him, shall be repassed by two thirds of the Senate and House of Representatives, according to the Rules and Limitations prescribed in the Case of a Bill.

SECTION 8

The Congress shall have Power To lay and collect Taxes, Duties, Imposts and Excises, to pay the Debts and provide for the common Defence and general Welfare of the United States; but all Duties, Imposts and Excises shall be uniform throughout the United States;

To borrow Money on the credit of the United States;

To regulate Commerce with foreign Nations, and

among the several States, and with the Indian Tribes;

To establish an uniform Rule of Naturalization, and uniform Laws on the subject of Bankruptcies throughout the United States;

To coin Money, regulate the Value thereof, and of foreign Coin, and fix the Standard of Weights and Measures;

To provide for the Punishment of counterfeiting the Securities and current Coin of the United States;

To establish Post Offices and post Roads;

To promote the Progress of Science and useful Arts, by securing for limited Times to Authors and Inventors the exclusive Right to their respective Writings and Discoveries;

To constitute Tribunals inferior to the supreme Court;

To define and punish Piracies and Felonies committed on the high Seas, and Offences against the Law of Nations;

To declare War, grant Letters of Marque and Reprisal, and make Rules concerning Captures on Land and Water;

To raise and support Armies, but no Appropriation of Money to that Use shall be for a longer Term than two Years;

To provide and maintain a Navy;

To make Rules for the Government and Regulation of the land and naval Forces;

To provide for calling forth the Militia to execute the Laws of the Union, suppress Insurrections and repel Invasions;

To provide for organizing, arming, and disciplining, the Militia, and for governing such Part of them as may be employed in the Service of the United States, reserving to the States respectively, the Appointment of the Officers, and the Authority of training the Militia according to the discipline prescribed by Congress;

To exercise exclusive Legislation in all Cases whatsoever, over such District (not exceeding ten Miles square) as may, by Cession of particular States, and the Acceptance of Congress, become the Seat of the Government of the United States, and to exercise like Authority over all Places purchased by the Consent of the Legislature of the State in which the Same shall be, for the Erection of Forts, Magazines, Arsenals, dock-Yards, and other needful Buildings;--And

To make all Laws which shall be necessary and proper for carrying into Execution the foregoing Powers, and all other Powers vested by this Constitution in the Government of the United States, or in any Department or Officer thereof.

SECTION 9

The Migration or Importation of such Persons as any of the States now existing shall think proper to admit, shall not be prohibited by the Congress prior to the Year one thousand eight hundred and eight, but a Tax or duty may be imposed on such Importation, not exceeding ten dollars for each Person.

The Privilege of the Writ of Habeas Corpus shall not be suspended, unless when in Cases of Rebellion or Invasion the public Safety may require it.

No Bill of Attainder or ex post facto Law shall be passed.

No Capitation, or other direct, Tax shall be laid, unless in Proportion to the Census or Enumeration herein before directed to be taken.

No Tax or Duty shall be laid on Articles exported from any State.

No Preference shall be given by any Regulation of Commerce or Revenue to the Ports of one State over those of another: nor shall Vessels bound to, or from, one State, be obliged to enter, clear, or pay Duties in another.

No Money shall be drawn from the Treasury, but in Consequence of Appropriations made by Law; and a regular Statement and Account of the Receipts and Expenditures of all public Money shall be published from time to time.

No Title of Nobility shall be granted by the United States: And no Person holding any Office of Profit or Trust under them, shall, without the Consent of the Congress, accept of any present, Emolument, Office, or Title, of any kind whatever, from any King, Prince, or foreign State.

SECTION 10

No State shall enter into any Treaty, Alliance, or Confederation; grant Letters of Marque and Reprisal; coin Money; emit Bills of Credit; make any Thing but gold and silver Coin a Tender in Payment of Debts; pass any Bill of Attainder, ex post facto Law, or Law impairing the Obligation of Contracts, or grant any Title of Nobility.

No State shall, without the Consent of the Congress, lay any Imposts or Duties on Imports or Exports, except what may be absolutely necessary for executing it's inspection Laws: and the net Produce of all Duties and Imposts, laid by any State on Imports or Exports, shall be for the Use of the Treasury of the United States; and all such Laws shall be subject to the Revision and Controul of the Congress.

No State shall, without the Consent of Congress, lay

TEA PARTY REVIVAL: THE CONSCIENCE OF A CONSERVATIVE REBORN

any Duty of Tonnage, keep Troops, or Ships of War in time of Peace, enter into any Agreement or Compact with another State, or with a foreign Power, or engage in War, unless actually invaded, or in such imminent Danger as will not admit of delay.

Article II

SECTION 1

The executive Power shall be vested in a President of the United States of America. He shall hold his Office during the Term of four Years, and, together with the Vice President, chosen for the same Term, be elected, as follows

Each State shall appoint, in such Manner as the Legislature thereof may direct, a Number of Electors, equal to the whole Number of Senators and Representatives to which the State may be entitled in the Congress: but no Senator or Representative, or Person holding an Office of Trust or Profit under the United States, shall be appointed an Elector.

The Electors shall meet in their respective States, and vote by Ballot for two Persons, of whom one at least shall not be an Inhabitant of the same State with themselves. And they shall make a List of all the Persons voted for, and of the Number of Votes for each; which List they shall sign and certify, and transmit sealed to the Seat of the Government of the United States, directed to the President of the Senate. The President of the Senate shall, in the Presence of the Senate and House of Representatives, open all the Certificates, and the Votes shall then be counted. The Person having the greatest Number of Votes shall be the President, if such Number be a Majority of the whole Number of Electors appointed; and if there be more than one who have such Majority, and have an equal Number of Votes, then the House of Representatives shall immediately chuse by Ballot one of them for President; and if no Person have a Majority, then from the five highest on the List the said House shall in like Manner chuse the President. But in chusing the President, the Votes shall be taken by States, the Representation from each State having one Vote; A quorum for this Purpose shall consist of a Member or Members from two thirds of the States, and a Majority of all the States shall be necessary to a Choice. In every Case, after the Choice of the President, the Person having the greatest Number of Votes of the Electors shall be the Vice President. But if there should remain two or more who have equal Votes, the Senate shall chuse from them by Ballot the Vice President.

The Congress may determine the Time of chusing the Electors, and the Day on which they shall give their Votes; which Day shall be the same throughout the United States.

No Person except a natural born Citizen, or a Citizen of the United States, at the time of the Adoption of this Constitution, shall be eligible to the Office of President; neither shall any Person be eligible to that Office who shall not have attained to the Age of thirty five Years, and been fourteen Years a Resident within the United States.

In Case of the Removal of the President from Office, or of his Death, Resignation, or Inability to discharge the Powers and Duties of the said Office, the Same shall devolve on the Vice President, and the Congress may by Law provide for the Case of Removal, Death, Resignation or Inability, both of the President and Vice President, declaring what Officer shall then act as President, and such Officer shall act accordingly, until the Disability be removed, or a President shall be elected.

The President shall, at stated Times, receive for his Services, a Compensation, which shall neither be encreased nor diminished during the Period for which he shall have been elected, and he shall not receive within that Period any other Emolument from the United States, or any of them.

Before he enter on the Execution of his Office, he shall take the following Oath or Affirmation:--"I do solemnly swear (or affirm) that I will faithfully execute the Office of President of the United States, and will to the best of my Ability, preserve, protect and defend the Constitution of the United States."

SECTION 2

The President shall be Commander in Chief of the Army and Navy of the United States, and of the Militia of the several States, when called into the actual Service of the United States; he may require the Opinion, in writing, of the principal Officer in each of the executive Departments, upon any Subject relating to the Duties of their respective Offices, and he shall have Power to grant Reprieves and Pardons for Offences against the United States, except in Cases of Impeachment.

He shall have Power, by and with the Advice and Consent of the Senate, to make Treaties, provided two thirds of the Senators present concur; and he shall nominate, and by and with the Advice and Consent of the Senate, shall appoint Ambassadors, other public Ministers and Consuls, Judges of the supreme Court, and all other Officers of the

United States, whose Appointments are not herein otherwise provided for, and which shall be established by Law: but the Congress may by Law vest the Appointment of such inferior Officers, as they think proper, in the President alone, in the Courts of Law, or in the Heads of Departments.

The President shall have Power to fill up all Vacancies that may happen during the Recess of the Senate, by granting Commissions which shall expire at the End of their next Session.

SECTION 3

He shall from time to time give to the Congress Information of the State of the Union, and recommend to their Consideration such Measures as he shall judge necessary and expedient; he may, on extraordinary Occasions, convene both Houses, or either of them, and in Case of Disagreement between them, with Respect to the Time of Adjournment, he may adjourn them to such Time as he shall think proper; he shall receive Ambassadors and other public Ministers; he shall take Care that the Laws be faithfully executed, and shall Commission all the Officers of the United States.

SECTION 4

The President, Vice President and all civil Officers of the United States, shall be removed from Office on Impeachment for, and Conviction of, Treason, Bribery, or other high Crimes and Misdemeanors.

Article III

SECTION 1

The judicial Power of the United States, shall be vested in one supreme Court, and in such inferior Courts as the Congress may from time to time ordain and establish. The Judges, both of the supreme and inferior Courts, shall hold their Offices during good Behaviour, and shall, at stated Times, receive for their Services, a Compensation, which shall not be diminished during their Continuance in Office.

SECTION 2

The judicial Power shall extend to all Cases, in Law and Equity, arising under this Constitution, the Laws of the United States, and Treaties made, or which shall be made, under their Authority; --to all Cases affecting Ambassadors, other public Ministers and Consuls; --to all Cases of admiralty and maritime Jurisdiction; --to Controversies to which the United States shall be a Party; --to Controversies between two or more States; --between a State and Citizens of another State; --between Citizens of different States, --between Citizens of the same State claiming Lands under Grants of different States, and between a State, or the Citizens thereof, and foreign States, Citizens or Subjects.

In all Cases affecting Ambassadors, other public Ministers and Consuls, and those in which a State shall be Party, the supreme Court shall have original Jurisdiction. In all the other Cases before mentioned, the supreme Court shall have appellate Jurisdiction, both as to Law and Fact, with such Exceptions, and under such Regulations as the

THE UNITED STATES CONSTITUTION ❧

Congress shall make.

The Trial of all Crimes, except in Cases of Impeachment, shall be by Jury; and such Trial shall be held in the State where the said Crimes shall have been committed; but when not committed within any State, the Trial shall be at such Place or Places as the Congress may by Law have directed.

SECTION 3

Treason against the United States, shall consist only in levying War against them, or in adhering to their Enemies, giving them Aid and Comfort. No Person shall be convicted of Treason unless on the Testimony of two Witnesses to the same overt Act, or on Confession in open Court.

The Congress shall have Power to declare the Punishment of Treason, but no Attainder of Treason shall work Corruption of Blood, or Forfeiture except during the Life of the Person attainted.

Article IV

SECTION 1

Full Faith and Credit shall be given in each State to the public Acts, Records, and judicial Proceedings of every other State. And the Congress may by general Laws prescribe the Manner in which such Acts, Records and Proceedings shall be proved, and the Effect thereof.

SECTION 2

The Citizens of each State shall be entitled to all Privileges and Immunities of Citizens in the several States.

A Person charged in any State with Treason, Felony, or other Crime, who shall flee from Justice, and be found in another State, shall on Demand of the executive Authority of the State from which he fled, be delivered up, to be removed to the State having Jurisdiction of the Crime.

No Person held to Service or Labour in one State, under the Laws thereof, escaping into another, shall, in Consequence of any Law or Regulation therein, be discharged from such Service or Labour, but shall be delivered up on Claim of the Party to whom such Service or Labour may be due.11

SECTION 3

New States may be admitted by the Congress into this Union; but no new State shall be formed or erected within the Jurisdiction of any other State; nor any State be formed by the Junction of two or more States, or Parts of States, without the Consent of the Legislatures of the States concerned as well as of the Congress.

The Congress shall have Power to dispose of and make all needful Rules and Regulations respecting the Territory or other Property belonging to the United States; and nothing in this Constitution shall be so construed as to Prejudice any Claims of the United States, or of any particular State.

SECTION 4

The United States shall guarantee to every State in this Union a Republican Form of Government, and shall protect each of them against Invasion; and on Application of the Legislature, or of the Executive (when the Legislature cannot be convened) against domestic Violence.

Article V

The Congress, whenever two thirds of both Houses shall deem it necessary, shall propose Amendments to this Constitution, or, on the Application of the Legislatures of two thirds of the several States, shall call a Convention for proposing Amendments, which, in either Case, shall be valid to all Intents and Purposes, as Part of this Constitution, when ratified by the Legislatures of three fourths of the several States, or by Conventions in three fourths thereof, as the one or the other Mode of Ratification may be proposed by the Congress; Provided that no Amendment which may be made prior to the Year One thousand eight hundred and eight shall in any Manner affect the first and fourth Clauses in the Ninth Section of the first Article; and that no State, without its Consent, shall be deprived of its equal Suffrage in the Senate.

Article VI

All Debts contracted and Engagements entered into, before the Adoption of this Constitution, shall be as valid against the United States under this Constitution, as under the Confederation. This Constitution, and the Laws of the United States which shall be made in Pursuance thereof; and all Treaties made, or which shall be made, under the Authority of the United States, shall be the supreme Law of the Land; and the Judges in every State shall be bound thereby, any Thing in the Constitution or Laws of any State to the Contrary notwithstanding.

The Senators and Representatives before mentioned, and the Members of the several State Legislatures, and all

executive and judicial Officers, both of the United States
and of the several States, shall be bound by Oath or
Affirmation, to support this Constitution; but no religious
Test shall ever be required as a Qualification to any Office
or public Trust under the United States.

Article VII

The Ratification of the Conventions of nine States,
shall be sufficient for the Establishment of this Constitution
between the States so ratifying the Same.

The Word "the", being interlined between the seventh
and eight Lines of the first Page, The Word "Thirty" being
partly written on an Erazure in the fifteenth Line of the first
Page. The Words "is tried" being interlined between the
thirty second and thirty third Lines of the first Page and the
Word "the" being interlined between the forty third and
forty fourth Lines of the second Page.

Done in Convention by the Unanimous Consent of the
States present the Seventeenth Day of September in the
Year of our Lord one thousand seven hundred and Eighty
seven and of the Independence of the United States of
America the Twelfth In witness whereof We have hereunto
subscribed our Names ... (signatures listed)

AMENDMENTS

AMENDMENTS

Amendment I

Congress shall make no law respecting an establishment of religion, or prohibiting the free exercise thereof; or abridging the freedom of speech, or of the press; or the right of the people peaceably to assemble, and to petition the Government for a redress of grievances.

Amendment II

A well regulated Militia, being necessary to the security of a free State, the right of the people to keep and bear Arms, shall not be infringed.

Amendment III

No Soldier shall, in time of peace be quartered in any house, without the consent of the Owner, nor in time of war, but in a manner to be prescribed by law.

Amendment IV

The right of the people to be secure in their persons, houses, papers, and effects, against unreasonable searches and seizures, shall not be violated, and no Warrants shall issue, but upon probable cause, supported by Oath or affirmation, and particularly describing the place to be searched, and the persons or things to be seized.

Amendment V

No person shall be held to answer for a capital, or otherwise infamous crime, unless on a presentment or indictment of a Grand Jury, except in cases arising in the land or naval forces, or in the Militia, when in actual service in time of War or public danger; nor shall any person be subject for the same offence to be twice put in jeopardy of life or limb; nor shall be compelled in any criminal case to be a witness against himself, nor be deprived of life, liberty, or property, without due process of law; nor shall private property be taken for public use, without just compensation.

Amendment VI

In all criminal prosecutions, the accused shall enjoy the right to a speedy and public trial, by an impartial jury of the State and district wherein the crime shall have been committed, which district shall have been previously ascertained by law, and to be informed of the nature and cause of the accusation; to be confronted with the witnesses against him; to have compulsory process for obtaining witnesses in his favor, and to have the Assistance of Counsel for his defence.

Amendment VII

In Suits at common law, where the value in controversy shall exceed twenty dollars, the right of trial by jury shall be preserved, and no fact tried by a jury, shall be otherwise re-examined in any Court of the United States, than according to the rules of the common law.

Amendment VIII

Excessive bail shall not be required, nor excessive fines imposed, nor cruel and unusual punishments inflicted.

Amendment IX

The enumeration in the Constitution, of certain rights, shall not be construed to deny or disparage others retained by the people.

Amendment X

The powers not delegated to the United States by the Constitution, nor prohibited by it to the States, are reserved to the States respectively, or to the people.

Amendment XI

The Judicial power of the United States shall not be construed to extend to any suit in law or equity, commenced or prosecuted against one of the United States by Citizens of another State, or by Citizens or Subjects of any Foreign State.

Amendment XII

The Electors shall meet in their respective states, and vote by ballot for President and Vice-President, one of whom, at least, shall not be an inhabitant of the same state with themselves; they shall name in their ballots the person voted for as President, and in distinct ballots the person voted for as Vice-President, and they shall make distinct lists of all persons voted for as President, and of all persons voted for as Vice-President, and of the number of votes for each, which lists they shall sign and certify, and transmit sealed to the seat of the government of the United States, directed to the President of the Senate;--The President of the Senate shall, in the presence of the Senate and House of Representatives, open all the certificates and the votes shall then be counted;--The person having the greatest number of votes for President, shall be the President, if such number be a majority of the whole number of Electors appointed; and if no person have such majority, then from the persons having the highest numbers not exceeding three on the list of those voted for as President, the House of Representatives shall choose immediately, by ballot, the President. But in choosing the President, the votes shall be taken by states, the representation from each state having one vote; a quorum for this purpose shall consist of a member or members from two-thirds of the states, and a majority of all the states shall be necessary to a choice. And if the House of Representatives shall not choose a

President whenever the right of choice shall devolve upon them, before the fourth day of March next following, then the Vice-President shall act as President, as in the case of the death or other constitutional disability of the President.14 --The person having the greatest number of votes as Vice-President, shall be the Vice-President, if such number be a majority of the whole number of Electors appointed, and if no person have a majority, then from the two highest numbers on the list, the Senate shall choose the Vice-President; a quorum for the purpose shall consist of two-thirds of the whole number of Senators, and a majority of the whole number shall be necessary to a choice. But no person constitutionally ineligible to the office of President shall be eligible to that of Vice-President of the United States.

Amendment XIII

Section 1. Neither slavery nor involuntary servitude, except as a punishment for crime whereof the party shall have been duly convicted, shall exist within the United States, or any place subject to their jurisdiction.

Section 2. Congress shall have power to enforce this article by appropriate legislation.

Amendment XIV

Section 1. All persons born or naturalized in the United States, and subject to the jurisdiction thereof, are citizens of the United States and of the State wherein they reside.

No State shall make or enforce any law which shall abridge the privileges or immunities of citizens of the United States; nor shall any State deprive any person of life, liberty, or property, without due process of law; nor deny to any person within its jurisdiction the equal protection of the laws.

Section 2. Representatives shall be apportioned among the several States according to their respective numbers, counting the whole number of persons in each State, excluding Indians not taxed. But when the right to vote at any election for the choice of electors for President and Vice President of the United States, Representatives in Congress, the Executive and Judicial officers of a State, or the members of the Legislature thereof, is denied to any of the male inhabitants of such State, being twenty-one years of age, and citizens of the United States, or in any way abridged, except for participation in rebellion, or other crime, the basis of representation therein shall be reduced in the proportion which the number of such male citizens shall bear to the whole number of male citizens twenty-one years of age in such State.

Section 3. No person shall be a Senator or Representative in Congress, or elector of President and Vice President, or hold any office, civil or military, under the United States, or under any State, who, having previously taken an oath, as a member of Congress, or as an officer of the United States, or as a member of any State legislature, or as an executive or judicial officer of any State, to support the Constitution of the United States, shall have engaged in insurrection or rebellion against the same, or given aid or comfort to the enemies thereof. But Congress may by a vote of two-thirds of each House, remove such disability.

Section 4. The validity of the public debt of the United States, authorized by law, including debts incurred for payment of pensions and bounties for services in suppressing insurrection or rebellion, shall not be questioned. But neither the United States nor any State shall assume or pay any debt or obligation incurred in aid of insurrection or rebellion against the United States, or any claim for the loss or emancipation of any slave; but all such debts, obligations and claims shall be held illegal and void.

Section 5. The Congress shall have power to enforce, by appropriate legislation, the provisions of this article.

Amendment XV

Section 1. The right of citizens of the United States to vote shall not be denied or abridged by the United States or by any State on account of race, color, or previous condition of servitude.

Section 2. The Congress shall have power to enforce this article by appropriate legislation.

Amendment XVI

The Congress shall have power to lay and collect taxes on incomes, from whatever source derived, without apportionment among the several States, and without regard to any census or enumeration.

Amendment XVII

The Senate of the United States shall be composed of two Senators from each State, elected by the people thereof, for six years; and each Senator shall have one vote. The electors in each State shall have the qualifications requisite for electors of the most numerous branch of the State legislatures.

When vacancies happen in the representation of any State in the Senate, the executive authority of such State shall issue writs of election to fill such vacancies: Provided, that the legislature of any State may empower the executive thereof to make temporary appointments until the people fill the vacancies by election as the legislature may direct.

This amendment shall not be so construed as to affect the election or term of any Senator chosen before it becomes valid as part of the Constitution.

Amendment XVIII

Section 1. After one year from the ratification of this article the manufacture, sale, or transportation of intoxicating liquors within, the importation thereof into, or the exportation thereof from the United States and all territory subject to the jurisdiction thereof for beverage purposes is hereby prohibited.

Section 2. The Congress and the several States shall have concurrent power to enforce this article by appropriate legislation.

Section 3. This article shall be inoperative unless it shall have been ratified as an amendment to the Constitution by the legislatures of the several States, as provided in the Constitution, within seven years from the date of the submission hereof to the States by the Congress.

Amendment XIX

The right of citizens of the United States to vote shall not be denied or abridged by the United States or by any State on account of sex.

Congress shall have power to enforce this article by appropriate legislation.

Amendment XX

Section 1. The terms of the President and Vice President shall end at noon on the 20th day of January, and the terms of Senators and Representatives at noon on the 3d day of January, of the years in which such terms would have ended if this article had not been ratified; and the terms of their successors shall then begin.

Section 2. The Congress shall assemble at least once in every year, and such meeting shall begin at noon on the 3d day of January, unless they shall by law appoint a different day.

Section 3. If, at the time fixed for the beginning of the term of the President, the President elect shall have died, the Vice President elect shall become President. If a President shall not have been chosen before the time fixed for the beginning of his term, or if the President elect shall have failed to qualify, then the Vice President elect shall act as President until a President shall have qualified; and the Congress may by law provide for the case wherein neither a President elect nor a Vice President elect shall have qualified, declaring who shall then act as President, or the manner in which one who is to act shall be selected, and such person shall act accordingly until a President or Vice President shall have qualified.

Section 4. The Congress may by law provide for the case of the death of any of the persons from whom the House of Representatives may choose a President whenever the right of choice shall have devolved upon them, and for the case of the death of any of the persons from whom the Senate may choose a Vice President whenever the right of choice shall have devolved upon them.

Section 5. Sections 1 and 2 shall take effect on the 15th day of October following the ratification of this article.

Section 6. This article shall be inoperative unless it shall have been ratified as an amendment to the Constitution by the legislatures of three-fourths of the several States within seven years from the date of its submission.

Amendment XXI

Section 1. The eighteenth article of amendment to the Constitution of the United States is hereby repealed.

Section 2. The transportation or importation into any State, Territory, or possession of the United States for delivery or use therein of intoxicating liquors, in violation of the laws thereof, is hereby prohibited.

Section 3. This article shall be inoperative unless it shall have been ratified as an amendment to the Constitution by conventions in the several States, as provided in the Constitution, within seven years from the date of the submission hereof to the States by the Congress.

Amendment XXII

Section 1. No person shall be elected to the office of the President more than twice, and no person who has held the office of President, or acted as President, for more than two years of a term to which some other person was elected President shall be elected to the office of the President more than once. But this article shall not apply to any person holding the office of President when this article was proposed by the Congress, and shall not prevent any person who may be holding the office of President, or acting as President, during the term within which this article becomes operative from holding the office of President or acting as President during the remainder of such term.

Section 2. This article shall be inoperative unless it shall have been ratified as an amendment to the Constitution by the legislatures of three-fourths of the several states within seven years from the date of its submission to the states by the Congress.

Amendment XXIII

Section 1. The District constituting the seat of government of the United States shall appoint in such manner as the Congress may direct: A number of electors of President and Vice President equal to the whole number of Senators and Representatives in Congress to which the District would be entitled if it were a state, but in no event more than the least populous state; they shall be in addition to those appointed by the states, but they shall be considered, for the purposes of the election of President and Vice President, to be electors appointed by a state; and they shall meet in the District and perform such duties as provided by the twelfth article of amendment.

Section 2. The Congress shall have power to enforce this article by appropriate legislation.

Amendment XXIV

Section 1. The right of citizens of the United States to vote in any primary or other election for President or Vice President, for electors for President or Vice President, or for Senator or Representative in Congress, shall not be denied or abridged by the United States or any state by reason of failure to pay any poll tax or other tax.

Section 2. The Congress shall have power to enforce this article by appropriate legislation.

Amendment XXV

Section 1. In case of the removal of the President from office or of his death or resignation, the Vice President shall become President.

Section 2. Whenever there is a vacancy in the office of the Vice President, the President shall nominate a Vice President who shall take office upon confirmation by a majority vote of both Houses of Congress.

Section 3. Whenever the President transmits to the President pro tempore of the Senate and the Speaker of the House of Representatives his written declaration that he is unable to discharge the powers and duties of his office, and until he transmits to them a written declaration to the contrary, such powers and duties shall be discharged by the Vice President as Acting President.

Section 4. Whenever the Vice President and a majority of either the principal officers of the executive departments or of such other body as Congress may by law provide, transmit to the President pro tempore of the Senate and the Speaker of the House of Representatives their written declaration that the President is unable to discharge the powers and duties of his office, the Vice President shall immediately assume the powers and duties of the office as Acting President.

Thereafter, when the President transmits to the President pro tempore of the Senate and the Speaker of the House of Representatives his written declaration that no inability exists, he shall resume the powers and duties of his office unless the Vice President and a majority of either the principal officers of the executive department or of such other body as Congress may by law provide, transmit within four days to the President pro tempore of the Senate and the Speaker of the House of Representatives their written declaration that the President is unable to discharge the powers and duties of his office. Thereupon Congress shall decide the issue, assembling within forty-eight hours for that purpose if not in session. If the Congress, within twenty-one days after receipt of the latter written declaration, or, if Congress is not in session, within twenty-one days after Congress is required to assemble, determines by two-thirds vote of both Houses that the President is unable to discharge the powers and duties of his office, the Vice President shall continue to discharge the same as Acting President; otherwise, the President shall resume the powers and duties of his office.

Amendment XXVI

Section 1. The right of citizens of the United States, who are 18 years of age or older, to vote, shall not be denied or abridged by the United States or any state on account of age.

Section 2. The Congress shall have the power to enforce this article by appropriate legislation.

Amendment XXVII

No law varying the compensation for the services of the Senators and Representatives shall take effect until an election of Representatives shall have intervened.

LaVergne, TN USA
11 March 2010
175668LV00001B/2/P